To:

_____

I will always have hope.

Psalm 71:14

From:

_____

Hope for a Woman's Soul: Meditations to Energize Your Spirit
Copyright 2000 by New Life Clinics
ISBN 0-310-98010-0

Requests for information should be addressed to:
    Inspirio, the Gift Group of Zondervan
    Grand Rapids, Michigan 49530

Compiler: Doris Rikkers
Associate Editor: Molly Detweiler
Design Manager: Amy E. Langeler
Designer: Sherri L. Hoffman

Printed in China

01 02 03 / HK/ 6 5 4 3 2

Hope for a Woman's Soul

Meditations to Energize Your Spirit

inspirio

The gift group of Zondervan

Table of Contents

Part I: Hope to Fill Your Heart

Part II: Hope in God's Love

Laugh with the Lord

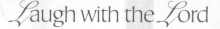

*J*esus knows about everything you're going through, and he has made arrangements for you to look back on it—and laugh. He is going to bring laughter and liberty into your circumstances. Wherever Jesus is, there's a party going on. His grace is the yeast that makes hope and joy rise in your heart.

Do you wonder what makes me qualified to dispense this "theology of laughter"? The heat got turned up in my family over a nine-year period. I lost a son in Vietnam, and another to a drunk driver. My third son entered a life of homosexuality and was estranged from us for many years. It's been tough. Believe me, my struggles would make a perky geranium wilt. But you know what I learned? Grace is stronger than gravity! When you're falling down, down, down, it's not a question of how far you fall, but how high you bounce.

Grace is all around you. No, life won't ever be perfect. Even in the land of milk and honey you can get kicked by a cow or stung by a bee. But when that happens, you can laugh with the Lord by your side.

BARBARA JOHNSON

*Y*ou may feel there are times in life that simply will not yield even an ounce of humor. May I suggest that during those seemingly interminable times of pain, you fight to see beyond the restrictive confines of the immediate; remind yourself that those moments will not last forever. Whatever it is that threatens to crush your spirit and claim your joy today will not necessarily be there tomorrow, next month, or next year. Life moves forward and circumstances change. You will not always be in a pit! That reminder in itself brings respite to the soul. From there perhaps a glimmer of light can seep through the darkness, enabling you to search out that seemingly elusive but spirit-lifting smile or laugh that helps you regain control.

MARILYN MEBERG

*M*editations for *L*aughing with the *L*ord

*O*ur mouths were filled with laughter, our tongues with songs of joy.... The LORD has done great things for us, and we are filled with joy.

Psalm 126:2–3

*J*esus said, "Blessed are you who weep now, for you will laugh."

Luke 6:21

A wife of noble character who can find? She is worth far more than rubies.... She is clothed with strength and dignity; she can laugh at the days to come.

Proverbs 31:10, 25

God Is in Control

❧

*G*od didn't go halfway when he went to work on my behalf. He did it all. Even when I couldn't feel him, even when I couldn't sense him, even when I wasn't holding on to him anymore, God worked on my behalf. He didn't need me to do a thing!

When I faced far worse than my worst imaginings, something unexpected and wonderful happened. I realized that God is in control and God is good—even when bad things happen in our lives.

Even though I didn't know what I might have to go through next, I could rest and accept it. Because now I knew that when I let go, I would fall into the strong hands of God.

JAN DRAVECKY

*E*very day we are blessed with opportunities to unwrap God's grace in our scary moments. Every day we witness miracles that we know no human could perform—miracles like being able to breath, walk, talk, move, see, think, taste, and touch. Evidence of God's presence and power is all around us in the universe—the sun, the stars, the birth of each new day. And yet, we continue to search for peace outside of Jesus, even when he is with us moment by moment on our journey.

When stormy weather rolls in around you, cry out to Jesus. No climactic change in your life is distressing or surprising to him. Listen to his still small voice as he whispers to you, "Why are you so afraid? Do you still have no faith?" When the gale is raging, you can be assured that he is standing by, speaking peace to your soul. Even the wind and the waves obey his will.

Thelma Wells

Meditations on
God Is in Control

*A*ll the ends of the earth will remember and turn to the LORD, and all the families of the nations will bow down before him, for dominion belongs to the LORD and he rules over the nations.

Psalm 22:27–28

*B*y Christ all things were created: things in heaven and on earth, visible and invisible, whether thrones or powers or rulers or authorities; all things were created by him and for him. He is before all things, and in him all things hold together.

Colossians 1:16–17

*Y*our kingdom, O LORD, is an everlasting kingdom, and your dominion endures through all generations. The LORD is faithful to all his promises and loving toward all he has made.

Psalm 145:13

Trust in the Lord

❧

*E*verybody experiences difficult situations in life. Everybody. Things that make us want to scream out or give up. Deprivations. Sacrifices. Losses. Misunderstandings. But isn't there some way for the Christian to respond without getting mad at God? Otherwise, what's the good of our faith? There has to be some key to being joyful in the midst of discouraging circumstances and crabby people. What is it?

It's taking God at his Word. It's believing he will do what he says, no matter how things look or how we feel. Nobody said it would be easy. If you find any Scripture that even hints that life will be easy, call me collect. Please. But I can tell you now . . . it ain't in there! However, trusting God with everything we have, everything we are, every problem that is ours, every loss we endure, every battle we face, every person who disappoints us—with thanksgiving—gives us the grace to come through it with flying colors.

LUCI SWINDOLL

So many things can trouble our hearts. Unpaid bills. A frightening medical prognosis. Loss of a job. The death of a loved one. Upcoming surgery. An unexpected move. An argument with a close friend. A savage rumor. A church dispute.

The world is full of "heart troublers," and it always will be. Yet Jesus does not want our hearts to remain troubled. And he does not expect us to deal with those troubles so much by ignoring them as by turning toward him. As he said to his anxious disciples in John 14:1, "Trust in God, trust also in me."

JAN DRAVECKY

Meditations for Trusting in the Lord

Trust in the LORD with all your heart and lean not on your own understanding; in all your ways acknowledge him, and he will make your paths straight.

Proverbs 3:5–6

Jesus said, "Do not let your hearts be troubled. Trust in God; trust also in me. . . . I am the way and the truth and the life. No one comes to the Father except through me."

John 14:1, 6

The LORD is good, a refuge in times of trouble. He cares for those who trust in him.

Nahum 1:7

Hope for Everyday

❧

God has given me much on this earth to enjoy. I love the joy on my son's face each evening as he gets ready for his bath. He looks at me and grins as he sees all his friends lined up along the side of the bath waiting for him in a long . . . long . . . long line. He picks up each one, says "hello," and throws it into the soapy deep. When he's finally fast asleep, I gather up all his stuff and put it to one side.

Perhaps there's a lesson for all of us there. The psalmist David writes that in the midst of the stress and confusion of everyday life, God has made known to him the path of life.

So each night now as I gather up my little lamb's bath mates and drop them into the boat, I also gather up the concerns and cares of the day that have filled my heart. Putting them to one side, I make room for Christ, the incarnation of grace. I stop to take notice of the gift of his presence. And he fills me with joy.

SHEILA WALSH

Some of us are like cats; we don't know what we want, but we want more of it. Others are like dogs; we don't want much, and we are overjoyed when we get it. Regardless of our personality type or temperament, our Creator takes great delight in lavishing his extravagant grace upon us.

Sometimes grace comes as wisdom—or an empty parking space, a pat on the back, a beautiful sunset, an unexpected act of kindness. Grace might mean finding your lost dog, running into an old friend at the mall, or hearing a wacky joke that doubles you over with laughter. Grace is when the customer service department refunds your money, sends you another item without charge, even hands you a certificate for $10 off on your next purchase, then asks, "Is that satisfactory?" Grace turns the corners of your mouth up when things in life are trying to turn them down.

BARBARA JOHNSON

Meditations on
Hope for Everyday

You have made known to me the path of life; you will fill me with joy in your presence, with eternal pleasures at your right hand.

Psalm 16:11

I rise before dawn and cry for help; I have put my hope in your word. My eyes stay open through the watches of the night, that I may meditate on your promises. . . . You are near, O LORD, and all your commands are true.

Psalm 119:147–148, 151

Jesus said, "Surely I am with you always, to the very end of the age."

Matthew 28:20

Every good and perfect gift is from above, coming down from the Father of the heavenly lights, who does not change like shifting shadows.

James 1:17

Just Be Yourself

❧

Sometimes the hardest thing in life is being ourselves. We so want to be somebody else. For years I sang with the Dallas Opera chorus, playing the part of other people. It was great. I wore wigs, corsets, fake eyelashes, heavy makeup, and costumes in order to become a waitress or a factory worker, a nun, courtesan, schoolteacher, soldier, . . . dancer, or lady-in-waiting. Whatever was called for, I became that. Interestingly, even my friends in the chorus used to say, "My favorite thing about all this is that I don't have to be me."

The next time you stand in front of a mirror and want to scream, try to remember that God made that face. That smile. Those big eyes, crooked teeth, and chubby cheeks. You are his creation, called to reflect him. Spiritual transformation doesn't come from a diet program, a bottle, a makeover, or mask. It comes from an intimate relationship with the Savior. Because of his gracious nature, he looks beyond our snaggle-toothed grin and appreciates us for who we really are. So we can, too.

LUCI SWINDOLL

*H*oney, if you are trying to be something you know you aren't, if you are trying to do things you know you have little ability, patience, passion, commitment, and tolerance for, cut it out! Be yourself! The great thing about real authority is that God gives me one thing to do, somebody else another, somebody else something else; or he may give us the same talent but have us exhibit it in different ways. Blending our authority with other people's authority creates the kind of kingdom on earth that personifies God's kingdom in heaven. The reason Lucifer was kicked out of heaven was that he tried to usurp God's authority and be something he wasn't. How very stupid when he had the fourth best position in heaven! His jealousy and rebellion cost him his position, his beauty, his ability to make angelic music, and his intimacy with God. When we operate outside of our authority, we experience similar breakdowns.

But that doesn't have to happen to you. Just be who you are, what you are, how you are, the way God made you. It is his grace that creates in you the talents, inclinations, knowledge and *pleasure* to be yourself. Grace empowers you to perform the tasks God has given you on earth, and to enjoy what he has called you to do.

THELMA WELLS

21

Meditations on Being Yourself

The LORD does not look at the things man looks at. Man looks at the outward appearance, but the LORD looks at the heart.

&❧ 1 Samuel 16:7

Now the body is not made up of one part but of many. . . . If the whole body were an eye, where would the sense of hearing be? If the whole body were an ear, where would the sense of smell be? But in fact God has arranged the parts in the body, every one of them, just as he wanted them to be.

&❧ 1 Corinthians 12:14, 17–18

Light at the End of the Tunnel

❧

Through it all—the chemo, the radiation, the nausea, and even those moments of fear—my husband Ken's humor prevailed. In fact, on the human level, his humor lightened many heavy moments. And that is what we all need to explore. We can be of good cheer when life hands us bad stuff. We can choose to see amusing moments in the midst of confusing and dark times. That choice does not make the confusing and dark times disappear, but it strengthens us as well as lightens our load so that we are more capable of coping. It never ceases to amaze me what load-lifters cheer and humor are. And Ken was very good at this cheerful business.

MARILYN MEBERG

*A*re you walking in the dark? Are the stars in your universe covered by clouds? Is there no light at the end of your tunnel—or do you see the headlight of an oncoming train?

Be still. Get quiet. What's that you hear? In your darkest hours, listen to Jesus saying, "Been there. Done that!"

Jesus, by the grace of God, has tasted what you are tasting, felt what your are feeling, looked into the blackest pit and prayed, "My Father, if it is possible, may this cup be taken from me" (Matthew 26:39). Jesus knows that clutch of fear in the night, the pain of sharp rocks under bare feet while dragging up a mountainside that nobody walked before. He knows the sound of that whistle from the oncoming train! Grace is God's gift in your darkness. Jesus is grace personified.

Are you going through a difficult struggle? Sit down and hold God's gift of grace in your lap. Slowly untie the ribbons. Now remove the lid on the box. Reach beneath the tissue paper. It's party time! In the middle of your trial, God has prepared a celebration. Jesus triumphed over the worst and now he will help you to do the same.

BARBARA JOHNSON

Meditations on Light at the End of the Tunnel

My God turns my darkness into light.

🌿 Psalm 18:28

The LORD is my strength and my shield; my heart trusts in him, and I am helped. My heart leaps for joy and I will give thanks to him in song.

🌿 Psalm 28:7

Thanks be to God! He gives us the victory through our Lord Jesus Christ. Therefore, . . . stand firm. Let nothing move you. Always give yourselves fully to the work of the Lord, because you know that your labor in the Lord is not in vain.

🌿 1 Corinthians 15:57–58

God's Agenda

*I*t's important to remember that God's agenda is the only right and perfect one and we can trust his plan completely. He guides us and gives us insight through his Word and through prayer and meditation. There will always be those who want to push their ideas in your face and expect you to embrace them, and some of them are right and good, but they should be examined carefully in light of God's Word and his plan for our lives. We must learn to recognize those who are "full of hot air!"

SUE BUCHANAN

*E*very now and then, I need to be reminded of who takes care of me and who is in charge of all the events in my life. When I'm skipping lithely across the high wire, congratulating myself on my confidence and skill, it's easy to forget who my safety net is. Fortunately, God doesn't let me be the star of the show from start to finish. Sometimes he turns things completely upside down so that what is happening does not make sense to me at all! In fact, I lose my balance completely, and I'm forced to cling to him and rest in his peace that passes understanding.

You may find yourself in the middle of circumstances that don't make sense to you. You may be surrounded by people who would never be your choice. Possibly God is reminding you that "the battle is the Lord's" and the way he wins battles is often through people and events we'd never even think of, much less choose. Why does God do this? "So that no one anywhere can ever brag in the presence of God."

Oddly enough, that knowledge takes the pressure off of me. I can quit striving, plotting, maneuvering. I am not the star of the show; God is.

MARILYN MEBERG

Meditations on God's Agenda

In his heart a man plans his course, but the LORD determines his steps.

> Proverbs 16:9

The LORD will guide you always; he will satisfy your needs.

> Isaiah 58:11

Many are the plans in a man's heart, but it is the LORD's purpose that prevails.

> Proverbs 19:21

In Christ we were also chosen, having been predestined according to the plan of him who works out everything in conformity with the purpose of his will, in order that we, who were the first to hope in Christ, might be for the praise of his glory.

> Ephesians 1:11–12

Hope Through Prayer

Even though it is often difficult for us to pray when we find ourselves in the middle of great trials, that is exactly the time when we most need to pray. Every time we pray, whether it feels like it or not, we are brought into the very throne room of heaven. Jesus himself ushers our prayers into the presence of the Father, and that alone assures us that they will be heard and answered. Prayer is a matter of obedience, but it is also a matter of survival. Prayer is the lifeline of the soul, and we cannot afford to do without it.

So let us pray to the God who hears and answers. Jesus has promised he will see to it that our requests get God's personal attention.

JAN DRAVECKY

*G*od invites us to take all our concerns to him. He never qualifies those concerns as big ones or little ones. His Word says every concern of ours is a concern of his.

I have assumed his attitude toward us is one of immense care. But that doesn't mean I should toss daily trivia to him, does it? The trouble with my thinking is I don't know at what point of my "carings" to bring God into the picture. What constitutes the cutoff point between big and small?

The notion of bringing God into everything has nothing to do with trivializing him; it has to do with the privilege of partnering with him. When I include God on my wild washing-machine rides and as I mentally travel in circles with my computer and its attitude, I'm cheered by his companionship and the knowledge that I'm in partnership with him.

MARILYN MEBERG

Meditations on Hope through Prayer

God has surely listened and heard my voice in prayer. Praise be to God, who has not rejected my prayer or withheld his love from me!

≈❧ Psalm 66:19–20

The prayer of a righteous man is powerful and effective.

≈❧ James 5:16

Christ, Jesus, who died—more than that, who was raised to life—is at the right hand of God and is also interceding for us.

≈❧ Romans 8:34

Jesus said, "If you believe, you will receive whatever you ask for in prayer."

≈❧ Matthew 21:22

Hope in Times of Grief

❧

My friend, God's grace shows up in *all* our circumstances if we would but recognize it. When we experience grief and sorrow and things don't turn out the way we want them to, God has not left us. He gives us more and more grace when the burdens are greater and greater.

There are times in all of our lives when grief of some kind sweeps over our soul, and we find ourselves looking for answers and comfort. Isn't it wonderful to know that a loving God cares enough about what we're going through to reach down and stroke our brow, or hug us through the arms of other people, or kiss us with the sweetness of kind words. Or send us flowers. As my friend Barbara Johnson says, "God will wrap you in his comfort blanket." Let him hold you now.

THELMA WELLS

*L*et me remind you of several things that are true for those who follow after Christ.

1. God loves you.
2. Christ has already paid for your sins.
3. Your eternal home is secure with him in heaven.
4. There will come a day when every tear will be wiped away and every heart be made new.
5. You are not alone, for Christ is with you every moment of every day.
6. You are a child of the King of kings. That is your eternal identity.

I know that life can be hard sometimes, and I encourage you to take time to grieve your losses, but do not be defined by them. Use them by the grace and strength of God as stepping-stones to a deeper life, a life of peace, a life lived with a thankful heart.

SHEILA WALSH

Meditations on Hope in Times of Grief

Find rest, O my soul, in God alone; my hope comes from him. He alone is my rock and my salvation; he is my fortress, I will not be shaken.

> 🍀 Psalm 62:5–6

Our hope for you is firm, because we know that just as you share in our sufferings, so also you share in our comfort.

> 🍀 2 Corinthians 1:7

The LORD comforts his people and will have compassion on his afflicted ones.

> 🍀 Isaiah 49:13

You, O God, do see trouble and grief; you consider it to take it in hand.

> 🍀 Psalm 10:14

God Is Constant and True

As someone once said, hope is the feeling you have that the feeling you have isn't permanent! I find that especially comforting to remember when I'm flying on an airplane.

When the airplane suddenly dips and dances around the sky, I find myself looking around for the flight attendants. It's not that I need to ask them to explain what's happening, I just need to see their faces. When I'm searching their faces for signs of hope, I try not to remember that this is just part of their professionalism. At that moment, I need to believe that what I see on their faces reflects reality, not their training!

When our lives get bumpy, we start looking around for God. It's not that we expect him to explain why things are happening the way they are. We just need to remind ourselves that he is there, still in control. And everything's going to be all right—if not in this life, then certainly in the next! As believers, when we look around for hope, we find God, constant and true.

 BARBARA JOHNSON

*L*ife for most of us is not a steady-paced stroll through time, with a beginning, a middle, and an end, like a well-constructed play. It's filled with change. We change schools, careers, homes, relationships, and "images" almost as casually as our great-grandparents changed horses.

Not that all change is by choice. Tragedy strikes and our lives change forever. A marriage dissolves, and a woman, linked to her husband by a thousand threads, finds those threads snapped and wonders who she is. Cherished friendships change in character or another person's choice cuts directly across our own, bringing us where we never wanted to be.

For the believer, then, this question is vital: Is our God the Lord of change? Will he be with us *in* change, especially when it strains our trust to its limit.

In a threatened world, in the kaleidoscopic whirl of our life patterns, it can be enormously reassuring to remind ourselves that God is unchanging: "I the LORD do not change" (Malachi 3:6). "Jesus Christ is the same yesterday and today and forever" (Hebrews 13:8).

GINI ANDREWS

Meditations on God Is Constant and True

The plans of the LORD stand firm
forever, the purposes of his heart
through all generations.

         Psalm 33:11

God is not a man, that he should lie,
nor a son of man, that he should
change his mind. Does he speak and
then not act? Does he promise and
not fulfill?

         Numbers 23:19

I will sing of the LORD's great love
forever; with my mouth I will make
your faithfulness known through all
generations. I will declare that your
love stands firm forever, that you
established your faithfulness in
heaven itself.

         Psalm 89:1–2

Walk with God

❧

I was a prisoner; an emotional prisoner. For several years I was held hostage in my home by fear and anger. Not knowing how to deal with the inequities of life, I stuffed my splintered emotions. I wasn't courageous, nor did I know how to handle life's pressures. Still, in my extreme weakness, God extended his grace to me. I embraced grace like a balance bar and gradually got back on my feet. Then with my jaw set and my eyes focused, I took the first gutsy steps out of my home.

God wants you to experience his grace whether you have faced your life with courage or with cowardice. Grace is not about us; it is about God. He will meet you wherever you are to help you take the next gutsy step. Understanding God's grace and appreciating it will change your approach to life's pressures. You will begin to see the injustices as opportunities for you to watch God at work.

By the way, God is not often in a hurry to move us on before we benefit deeply from our experiences. So don't be disheartened when others forget your long, hard struggles. He will never forget . . . and his grace will exalt you in due time.

PATSY CLAIRMONT

In heavenly love abiding,
No change my heart shall fear;
And safe is such confiding,
For nothing changes here.
The storm may roar without me,
My heart may low be laid,
But God is round about me,
And can I be dismayed?

Whenever he may guide me,
No fear shall turn me back;
My Shepherd is beside me,
And nothing shall I lack.
His wisdom ever waketh,
His sight is never dim;
He knows the way he taketh,
And I will walk with him.

Green pastures are before me,
Which yet I have not seen;
Bright skies will soon be o'er me,
Where darkest clouds have been.
My hope I cannot measure,
My path to life is free;
My Savior is my treasure,
And he will walk with me.

ANNA L. WARING

Meditations on Walking with God

I will walk among you and be your God, and you will be my people.

🕊 Leviticus 26:12

When you walk, your steps will not be hampered; when you run, you will not stumble.

🕊 Proverbs 4:12

Those who hope in the LORD will renew their strength. They will soar on wings like eagles; they will run and not grow weary, they will walk and not be faint.

🕊 Isaiah 40:31

Be strong and courageous. Do not be afraid or terrified . . . for the LORD your God goes with you; he will never leave you nor forsake you.

🕊 Deuteronomy 31:6

Running Away

❧

All of us have times when we feel like running away from home. "Just the thought of *running* is enough to change my mind!" a friend told me. But there are better reasons for not running. Troubles are often the tools God uses to cultivate the fruit of his grace in our lives. Our challenge is to accept that grace, to obey, and to serve.

Like the widow at Zarephath, whose jug of oil never ran out, you can never use up grace. When you think you're fresh out of grace, God gives you more. When you use what you have, look at the jug—the more you use, the more you get!

What is it that *you* need today? Are you being tempted to despair? To throw in the towel? To lose hope? To roll over and die? God is watching in the wings. He says, "Bake a cake before you chuck it all." Face your fears. Unwrap the grace in this moment. Expect a miracle. God has a plan. Be there when he stops by. He's got a miracle of grace in store, just for you.

BARBARA JOHNSON

*M*ost of us know what we *don't* want in life, but not so many of us know what we *do* want. And not having what we want, or not wanting what we have, leads to discontentment, if not hopelessness and despair. But I've learned that there are ways around these feelings. We can run away. We can keep accumulating—things, people, experiences— trying to find what we *might* want, what's missing. We can learn to pretend that we're completely-satisfied-thank-you. Or . . . we can do the one and only thing that works: turn to God and his Word. It is he who brings about real change in our lives. And how does he do that? By giving us hope.

The person who has a relationship with the God of the universe, through his Son Jesus Christ, can know for sure that his hope is secure. It will not come up short.

LUCI SWINDOLL

Meditations on Running Away

Where can I go from your Spirit? Where can I flee from your presence? If I go up to the heavens, you are there; if I make my bed in the depths, you are there. If I rise on the wings of the dawn, if I settle on the far side of the sea, even there your hand will guide me, your right hand will hold me fast.

≈❧ Psalm 139:7–10

Consider it pure joy . . . whenever you face trials of many kinds, because you know that the testing of your faith develops perseverance. Perseverance must finish its work so that you may be mature and complete, not lacking anything.

≈❧ James 1:2–4

Just As I Am

❧

I spent several years as a dismal prisoner in my home. My outlook on life had become warped. I viewed myself through the distortion of fear, and believe me, fear both controls and distorts. My snarled emotions then kept me from embracing the truth that in Christ I had "a future and a hope." Instead of my faith buoying my spirit, I dragged my saggy beliefs around as if they were a bagful of rocks. That is, until I began to view myself through the liberating reflection of God's Word. The Bible is a hope-full mirror that, yes, exposes the truth about yesterday and today, but not without improving our outlook on tomorrow.

My friends have also been hope bearers for me by reflecting Christ's love both in my early years of struggle and today. They have been like zany mirrors for me in that they assure me that my cockeyed reflection is both accurate and acceptable. I am irregular in many ways, but the Lord is not surprised by the shape I'm in nor is he put off by my teetering style or that of my friends.

PATSY CLAIRMONT

I think it would be a good idea if you could lose a few pounds," my manager suggested. "I'm enrolling you in a clinic for two weeks. They will exercise you and put you on a strict diet. You'll be a new woman!"

For the next two weeks, I was wrapped, pummeled and starved till I looked like a leftover turkey. Then came D-Day, I stood on the scale—I had gained four pounds!

I hated myself. I was so ashamed that I had no willpower. I felt ugly and unlovable. I imagined when people looked at me they saw a fat, unattractive girl because that's what I saw in the bathroom mirror.

When you look in a mirror, what do you see? Do you zero in on a crooked nose, a blemish, a sagging jaw, tired eyes packing their own bags? I encourage you as a fellow traveler to cherish and celebrate the gift of grace that calls you to draw near, to let go of your obsession with the shell of your life, and to fall more in love with Jesus. As women who have been drawn close to the heart of God by the embrace of Christ, you and I have the best reason of all to rejoice.

SHEILA WALSH

Meditations on Just as I Am

God demonstrates his own love for us in this: While we were still sinners, Christ died for us.

> Romans 5:8

Speak and act as those who are going to be judged by the law that gives freedom, because judgment without mercy will be shown to anyone who has not been merciful. Mercy triumphs over judgment!

> James 2:12–13

Good and upright is the LORD; therefore he instructs sinners in his ways.

> Psalm 25:8

New Beginnings

✿

*E*ach one of us needs a new beginning at some point or other. But it needn't come with a bang of fireworks or a streaking comet. New beginnings often come slowly. They may even sneak up on you—like a tiny ray of sun slipping out from beneath a black cloud. You can be inspired by the smallest things, so keep your eyes open.

Consider these: A tea kettle singing on the stove inspired the steam engine. A shirt waving on a clothesline inspired the balloon. A spider web strung across a garden path inspired the suspension bridge. God will use the simplest realities to inspire something bigger and better in your life.

God has much greater ambitions for us than we have for ourselves. He laughs at our paltry plans, then plots to surprise us with the greatness of his grace. Of course, we have to learn to live with the rain and the fog while we're waiting for our skies to clear up and God's glory to be revealed. But rest your hope upon the grace that will crown your life when Jesus' plan unfolds.

BARBARA JOHNSON

$\mathcal{A}$ single lonely bird hovered over a submerged world. Nowhere could she find a place to hold on to. She found no rest. Noah waited for her return. When the bird came, she found an outstretched hand, ready to take her into the safety of the ark. Together they were on their way to a new future.

We can be compared with this dove. We feel lonely and forsaken. We flutter around in a world that increasingly offers less to hold on to in every way. We see little hope for humanity. Spiritually and emotionally we find no rest.

Yet there is Someone who cares about us, who watches closely for each individual: God! Through him we can find rest in spite of the catastrophes that harass the world. He offers us a place to stand, and hope, even in an apparently lost world. He offers a new beginning to those of us who return to him.

GIEN KARSSEN

Meditations on New Beginnings

I saw the Holy City, the new Jerusalem, coming down out of heaven from God, prepared as a bride beautifully dressed for her husband. . . . God who was seated on the throne said, "I am making everything new!"

    ❧ Revelation 21:2, 5

*P*raise be to the God and Father of our Lord Jesus Christ! In his great mercy he has given us new birth into a living hope through the resurrection of Jesus Christ from the dead, and into an inheritance that can never perish, spoil or fade—kept in heaven for you.

    ❧ 1 Peter 1:3–4

*I*f anyone is in Christ, he is a new creation; the old has gone, the new has come!

    ❧ 2 Corinthians 5:17

The Power of Hope

※❧

*H*ope is perhaps the most precious commodity we have. Hope has the power to splash living colors on bleak and barren landscapes, to fill empty chests with golden treasures, and to infuse life and vitality where before there was only death and despair.

Jesus knew well the awesome power of hope, and that is why he poured an ocean of it on his disciples shortly before he was taken away to be crucified. And yet how honestly he poured! Who among us would begin a warm bath of hope with a bracing shower of reality? Yet that is just what the Master did. Before he lavished on his men this gift of hope, he declared to them why they would need it so badly. "I tell you the truth," he said, "you will weep and mourn . . . you will grieve."

Jesus is always candid with his followers, both then and now. He knows the end from the beginning and is aware that the middle is often filled with pain, tears, and grief.

And yet that is not the whole story! For the world Jesus created is decidedly not a world without hope. In fact, it's fairly crammed with the stuff!

※ DAVE AND JAN DRAVECKY

*W*hile flying to a conference recently, I was leafing through the airline's magazine which has items you can purchase through a catalog. I spied a darling ad showing a black umbrella. The description said, "Gray skies are gonna clear up!" The umbrella opened to reveal a blue sky with white fluffy clouds floating by. It was like moving out from under dismal rain clouds to a clear bright day at the touch of a button.

I had to order that umbrella, of course, because it was such an encouragement to me! When it arrived in the mail, it was even better than depicted in the advertisement. It brought inspiration and joy into my gloomy days.

None of us can avoid the gray skies and dreariness in life. At times we get absolutely drenched with troubles. But you know what? They're gonna clear up! Nothing lasts forever. The stuff we go through is only temporary. There will be lots of clearings along the way. And one day we will enjoy blue skies forever.

Barbara Johnson

Meditations on the Power of Hope

I pray . . . that the eyes of your heart may be enlightened in order that you may know the hope to which God has called you, the riches of his glorious inheritance in the saints, and his incomparably great power for us who believe.

❧ Ephesians 1:18–19

The LORD performs wonders that cannot be fathomed, miracles that cannot be counted. He bestows rain on the earth; he sends water upon the countryside. The lowly he sets on high, and those who mourn are lifted to safety.

❧ Job 5:9–11

What was glorious has no glory now in comparison with the surpassing glory. And if what was fading away came with glory, how much greater is the glory of that which lasts! Therefore, since we have such a hope, we are very bold.

❧ 2 Corinthians 3:10–12

Leave It with God

My mother was serious about hoping in Christ, and her prayer life proved it. She was not a saint. I'm sure there were days when she even wanted to run away. But she learned how to rely on the ever-present grace of God, putting her faith constantly on him, holding fast to a hope that did not disappoint. I don't know why her children did the very thing she longed for them to do—certainly not because she did everything right all the time. My guess is simply that God answered her prayer. Her example of hoping in him makes me want to hang on, too, to the goodness of the God who loves me, regardless of mundane daily life and my own frailties.

LUCI SWINDOLL

$\mathscr{D}$o not be anxious about anything."
What a promise! This is an all-inclusive verse.
Do not worry about anything. Don't worry
about the children or your car payment or
your job or your health. Whatever is on your
heart and mind, bring it to the Lord in prayer
and in petition and do it with thanksgiving.
Thanksgiving is such an important part of the
process because it speaks to trust and confidence.

When we take our prayer requests to God
and then continue to worry, it is as if we are
saying, "Thanks so much for stopping to listen to me, but I'm not sure you can help." In
our souls we sense the dissonance in that
line of thinking. We believe that God is able
to do what he says he will do; why then is it
so difficult to rest in this promise? *Don't be
anxious about anything.*

SHEILA WALSH

Meditations on Leaving It with God

God is able to do immeasurably more than all we ask or imagine.

❧❧ Ephesians 3:20

Do not be anxious about anything, but in everything, by prayer and petition, with thanksgiving, present your requests to God. And the peace of God, which transcends all understanding, will guard your hearts and your minds in Christ Jesus.

❧❧ Philippians 4:6–7

Jesus said, "Do not worry, saying, 'What shall we eat?' or 'What shall we drink?' or 'What shall we wear?' . . . But seek first God's kingdom and his righteousness, and all these things will be given to you as well. Therefore do not worry about tomorrow, for tomorrow will worry about itself."

❧❧ Matthew 6:31, 33–34

God Working Through Us

*A*s a child of God, each of us has a divine call and destiny, and yet so often we are held back by fear and doubt. We are afraid of making a mistake, of looking foolish. We find it easy to believe that God can use someone else. But us? It requires a leap of faith to grasp hold of the truth that God can take us beyond our own abilities; we must simply trust him and keep pushing on through the night. The Word of God never says we mustn't make a mistake, but it has a lot to say about those who doubt.

It is easy to believe that God can use our lives when we see immediate results, when positive feedback encourages us to push on. It is hard to keep walking when we see little sign that what we are doing is making a difference.

Perhaps there is little immediate satisfaction in what you have been called to do, but if you will faithfully push on through the night the Lord is the one who carries a reward in his hands.

SHEILA WALSH

When I was a missionary in Vietnam, a missionary friend and I were invited by a Korean general to an important military ceremony. The only women amidst thousands of Korean, Vietnamese and American troops, we sat on the reviewing stand with the three-nation generals to watch the elaborate ceremonies.

Thoroughly mystified as to why we had been invited, we were conducted to the general's mess where we ate a sumptuous meal on crested china and gold-plated flatware.

Finally, at the end of the meal, the Korean general called for his interpreter and said to me, "I am sure you are wondering why I invited you here today!" He continued with this remarkable comment: "When I was a small boy in Korea, an American lady missionary led me to Jesus Christ, and I never had the opportunity to thank her. So wherever I go, I look up missionaries and honor them!"

There are no doubt many who have illuminated our paths through this life. As we are obedient to God's command there will be those whose lives we may brighten. Let your light so shine!

CHARLOTTE STEMPLE

Meditations on God Working Through Us

God, who said, "Let light shine out of darkness," made his light shine in our hearts to give us the light of the knowledge of the glory of God in the face of Christ. But we have this treasure in jars of clay to show that this all-surpassing power is from God and not from us.

2 Corinthians 4:6–7

Those who are wise will shine like the brightness of the heavens, and those who lead many to righteousness, like the stars for ever and ever.

Daniel 12:3

To those who by persistence in doing good seek glory, honor and immortality, God will give eternal life.

Romans 2:7

Hope at All Times

Suffering and sorrow are never welcome guests. They take us by surprise and squeeze our hearts, but I believe they are necessary to make the melody of our lives complete. It's possible to try to live your life in one color, protecting yourself from the full spectrum of human experience, but the sounds that emerge are a little hollow and one-dimensional.

We were made for the joy and laughter of the major keys and also for the pain and tears of the minor. Part of being fully alive to God is being willing to embrace all that he puts in our path. That includes the unexpected stones that scrape our souls, so that we can become more like him.

When I study the life of Christ, I sense a deep, rich symphony ascending to the heart of God—using every note and inflection. This is what we, too, were made for.

SHEILA WALSH

*H*ope is a precious gift of our salvation. Our only reliable hope is in what we cannot see or control: the outrageous faithfulness of God. Our responsibility to him as his children is to study his character so we will know, without a doubt, that whatever way he deals with our circumstances in life, it's the right way. Even when things don't work out the way we planned or desired, he is all-knowing, all-loving, the beginning and the ending. Hope is acting on the conviction that despite what we see with the natural eye, God is working in the spiritual realm to accomplish his perfect will in our lives. His hope does not disappoint!

God's Word declares hope. God's promises proclaim hope. We must think hope. Speak hope. Pray hope. Sing hope. Act out hope. Stand firm on hope. Share hope. In other words get our hopes up. Because hope has been given to us, we can expect the best, even in the worst conditions. Praise God!

THELMA WELLS

Meditations on Hope at All Times

Set your hope fully on the grace to be given you when Jesus Christ is revealed.

  1 Peter 1:13

Let the morning bring me word of your unfailing love, for I have put my trust in you, O LORD.

  Psalm 143:8

Let us then approach the throne of grace with confidence, so that we may receive mercy and find grace to help us in our time of need.

  Hebrews 4:16

Hope Defined

❧

*M*any of us have ideas about hope that are simply all wrong—totally contrary to what biblical hope is all about. Either we experience hope as mere wishful thinking or we cynically dismiss it as child's play.

A born-twice, Holy-Spirit-filled woman of God can do better! Hope for the Christian is much more than pie-in-the-sky wishful thinking. The dictionary defines hope as a verb of expectation—to "hope against hope," to actively and confidently expect fulfillment. Hope as a noun is defined as a confident expectation that a desire will be fulfilled. Hope as a virtue is described as the confidence with which a Christian looks for God's grace in this world and glory in the next.

Did you get the common denominator? Hope is all about placing our confidence in what we can't yet see, about having high expectations that, in spite of all appearances to the contrary, our deepest longings will be fulfilled. And as Christians, that's exactly what we can count on.

THELMA WELLS

So where do you go when you can't fix your life? The only place to go is back to the One who made you. You have a divine destiny, a purpose from God that no one else can fulfill. It begins with a risk. We have to find the courage to take all the pieces of our lives, our hopes and dreams back to the One who made us—and ask him who we are. Then he, like the watchmaker, will carefully and gently replace our broken parts, showing us what we are meant to be and giving us all that we need to live our lives according to our purpose and his plan.

SHEILA WALSH

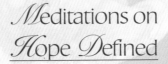
Meditations on Hope Defined

Faith is being sure of what we hope for and certain of what we do not see.

Hebrews 11:1

Hope that is seen is no hope at all. Who hopes for what he already has? But if we hope for what we do not yet have, we wait for it patiently.

Romans 8:24–25

I am the LORD, the God of all mankind. Is anything too hard for me?

Jeremiah 32:27

I will praise you forever for what you have done, O LORD; in your name I will hope, for your name is good.

Psalm 52:9

Meditation
on Hope

We rejoice in the hope of the glory of God. Not only so, but we also rejoice in our sufferings, because we know that suffering produces perseverance; perseverance, character; and character, hope. And hope does not disappoint us, because God has poured out his love into our hearts by the Holy Spirit, whom he has given us.

Romans 5:2–5

Hope
in
God's Love

God Is Here!

After four hundred years of silence following the close of the Old Testament, God showed up on the night shift, to the shepherds. In the voice of his archangel he proclaimed salvation to the boys on the hill.

This radical gift of grace shows us that God's love is based on nothing we have done, but on who he is. Do you think God looked down at a few shepherds under the stars and thought, "These are the only guys who have their act together. I think I'll break the news to them first." I don't think so. God so longed for us to get the message of grace that he chose to display his glory to people like you and me who try so hard and fail so often. He shows up to people who slip into the bathroom for a quick shot of something to deaden the pain of life. He shows up to all the broken, lonely people of the world with the Good News: God is here!

SHEILA WALSH

*C*an you imagine God's delight in us is so genuine, so spontaneous, so spirited that he exults over us by singing happy songs? Can you imagine that he not only lives among us (within us) and promises to give us victory, but also that he rejoices over us in great gladness? Who in your lifetime—past, present, or future—has ever been or will ever be so utterly in love with you?

Only God! Plain, simple, profound. That realization is enough to cause me to look up, up, up, and topple over with cheer-inducing, heartfelt gratitude.

So come on! Grab your robe and join the joyous choir. There's a lot more living, loving, and laughing to do. Sure, there's plenty of stuff in this world to steal your joy. But remember, you have Jesus, the Overcomer. You have a choice. You can choose cheer over fear.

MARILYN MEBERG

Meditations on God Is Here

The LORD *your God is with you, he is mighty to save. He will take great delight in you, he will quiet you with his love, he will rejoice over you with singing.*

🌺 Zephaniah 3:17

Surely God is my salvation; I will trust and not be afraid. The LORD*, the* LORD*, is my strength and my song; he has become my salvation.*

🌺 Isaiah 12:2

The virgin will be with child and will give birth to a son, and they will call him "Immanuel"—which means, "God with us."

🌺 Matthew 1:23

Grace, mercy and peace from God the Father and from Jesus Christ, the Father's Son, will be with us in truth and love.

🌺 2 John 1:3

Living the Abundant Life

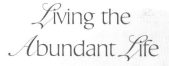

*G*od has proven himself the great provider just at the time of my friends' greatest need. One has lost a baby and her husband, one suffered clinical depression, one spent years a prisoner in her own home addicted to fear, one was the victim of tremendous racial abuse, one has lost two grown sons and was severely disappointed by the lifestyle of a third. What tragic circumstances in life. Enough heartache to bury a person. And yet, what brought these women of faith together? Joy. God's transforming grace enabled my friends to transcend life's greatest sorrows and emerge with testimonies of joy.

This unmerited favor from God not only secures our eternal salvation, but it also empowers us to keep walking steadily through life's trials and torments. Because we have received "so great a Grace," our lives are altogether different. We have the ability to live on a different plane. No longer do we merely survive, but we live fully; no longer endure but enjoy. God's outrageous grace has given us an abundant life.

LUCI SWINDOLL

I can remember a period in my life when I was flat broke. Sometimes I would have only a quarter in my purse. I kept that so if the car broke down or I needed to call someone on the phone, I could. At times I would have a pity party about my financial dilemma. But the party wouldn't last too long because I would begin to think about how blessed I was. I had two good arms, legs, eyes, ears, feet; I could think, work, give, love. When I'd begin thinking about how good God was to me and my family even in that desperate financial state, I would inevitably start praising him for what I had rather than lamenting over what I did not have.

Even though I had no tangible evidence, I was excited about what God was doing for me. I had faith to believe that he would not leave me poor—that in the supernatural realm he had already worked out his divine solutions to my problems.

THELMA WELLS

Meditations on Living the Abundant Life

If, by the trespass of the one man, death reigned through that one man, how much more will those who receive God's abundant provision of grace and of the gift of righteousness reign in life through the one man, Jesus Christ.

  Romans 5:17

Blessed are all who fear the LORD, who walk in his ways. You will eat the fruit of your labor; blessings and prosperity will be yours.

  Psalm 128:1–2

Jesus said, "I have come that they may have life, and have it to the full."

  John 10:10

The grace of our Lord was poured out on me abundantly, along with the faith and love that are in Christ Jesus.

  1 Timothy 1:14

Our Only Hope

I'm sure you have plenty of your own stories that showcase God's faithfulness. God has proved himself over and over in our lives; our hope in him is never empty. But when our minds start swinging from one negative thought to another, we find ourselves in danger of falling. The trapeze artist who loses concentration can easily miss connecting with her partner or the swinging bar. Yikes! Down on the net she goes. She may be embarrassed or a little shaken, but most of the time she is not seriously injured.

Jesus is like that net. He is always beneath us, waiting to catch us when we lose our concentration on him and miss the connections. He's our only real H.O.P.E.

H: Heavenly.
O: Omnipotent.
P: Powerful.
E: Everlasting Savior.

When we trust in him alone, life may still shake us up, but our spirit will be safe in the net of his love.

THELMA WELLS

My Hope is Built

My hope is built on nothing less
Than Jesus' blood and righteousness.
I dare not trust the sweetest frame,
But wholly trust in Jesus' Name.

On Christ the solid Rock I stand,
All other ground is sinking sand;
All other ground is sinking sand.

When darkness seems to hide His face,
I rest on His unchanging grace.
In every high and stormy gale,
My anchor holds within the veil.

His oath, His covenant, His blood,
Support me in the whelming flood.
When all around my soul gives way,
He then is all my Hope and Stay.

When He shall come with trumpet sound,
Oh may I then in Him be found.
Dressed in His righteousness alone,
Faultless to stand before the throne.

EDWARD MOTE

Meditations on Our Only Hope

Because Jesus lives forever, he has a permanent priesthood. Therefore he is able to save completely those who come to God through him, because he always lives to intercede for them.

    ❦ Hebrews 7:24–25

God did not send his Son into the world to condemn the world, but to save the world through him.

    ❦ John 3:17

If only for this life we have hope in Christ, we are to be pitied more than all men. But Christ has indeed been raised from the dead, the firstfruits of those who have fallen asleep. For since death came through a man, the resurrection of the dead comes also through a man.

    ❦ 1 Corinthians 15:19–21

Lost and Found

❧

I really can relate to being the lost sheep! If you've ever been lost in a parking garage, I think you can safely say you know what it feels like to be lost! I can say with pride that I always remember to take note of which door of what store I come in, so the problem is not getting back outside. It's remembering where I parked and what the car looks like.

I know what you're thinking! It's really silly to compare the biblical story of the lost sheep to being lost in the parking lot of a shopping mall with your arms full of bags. Maybe not. It seems like the Lord always uses something extremely basic to make his point.

It's so simple: He is our Shepherd, we are his sheep, and he doesn't think of us in bunches or herds or gaggles or flocks or swarms or prides (as in lions) or schools (as in fish), pods, coveys, packs, or droves. *Or even congregations, thank heavens!* He knows us as individuals and loves us so much he laid down his life: "I am the Good Shepherd. The good Shepherd lays down his life for the sheep."

🖌 Sue Buchanan

God makes no distinction on account of nationality, race, caste, or gender. He made us all and loves us equally. Christ came to remove every last wall of partition between us and his Father so that everybody who wants to can become part of his family. God's plan is for all of us to turn from our wicked ways and worship him. Even though we disobey his law, he has chosen to redeem us under the new covenant of Jesus Christ. He plans to rescue each one of us from our fate apart from him.

Dear friend, if you are lost, you can be found. No one is destined for the "unclaimed" bin at life's Lost and Found. Simply acknowledge your need for the Savior and honor God. It doesn't matter who you are or where you've been. That's why grace is so amazing. It saves wretches like me, like you.

THELMA WELLS

Meditations on Lost and Found

Jesus said, "The Son of Man came to seek and to save what was lost."

꧁ Luke 19:10

Jesus said, "Suppose one of you has a hundred sheep and loses one of them. Does he not leave the ninety-nine in the open country and go after the lost sheep until he finds it? And when he finds it, he joyfully puts it on his shoulders and goes home. Then he calls his friends and neighbors together and says, 'Rejoice with me; I have found my lost sheep.' I tell you that in the same way there will be more rejoicing in heaven over one sinner who repents than over ninety-nine righteous persons who do not need to repent."

꧁ Luke 15:4–7

God Is Faithful

❧

I used to have an answer for most problems in life. I had a lot to say on almost any subject. I now have fewer answers, and they might be reduced to the simple phrase, God is faithful. I don't say that lightly or without thought; I say it because I know it is true, and I have discovered that it is true no matter what is happening in my life. With confidence, I add these words to the end of the worst statements in the world: My child is sick and I don't know what to do . . . but God is faithful; I lost my job and I don't know how I will pay my bills . . . but God is faithful; my husband has left me and my heart is torn in two . . . but God is faithful.

I don't mean that he will wave a magic wand and everything will fall into place; far from it. What I mean is that if in the darkest times in our lives we will learn to keep turning our face toward him, he is faithful. Faithful to be with us, faithful to watch over us, faithful to work in us to make us the men and women we are called to be.

SHEILA WALSH

*S*omeday, perhaps, we will understand why God allows some seemingly inexplicable adversities to enter our lives. First Corinthians 13:12 promises us that, when we see God "face to face" and not as in a poor reflection, we shall know fully even as we are fully known. Of course, we will never be God and there will always be divine mysteries beyond our ability to comprehend. Yet someday the things that so perplex and bother us now may become clear, resulting in a vastly greater appreciation and love for the God who has called us his own dear children.

In the meanwhile, we can rest in the sure knowledge that God is faithful and that he has something in store for us that is quite beyond our comprehension. I for one am glad he did not try to tell us more than he has. My head is already spinning at the wonders he has revealed—and those are just the previews!

DAVE AND JAN DRAVECKY

Meditations on God Is Faithful

This I call to mind and therefore I have hope: Because of the LORD's great love we are not consumed, for his compassions never fail. They are new every morning; great is your faithfulness.

> Lamentations 3:21–23

Great are the works of the LORD; they are pondered by all who delight in them. Glorious and majestic are his deeds, and his righteousness endures forever. He has caused his wonders to be remembered; the LORD is gracious and compassionate. He provides food for those who fear him; he remembers his covenant forever. He has shown his people the power of his works, giving them the lands of other nations. The works of his hands are faithful and just; all his precepts are trustworthy. They are steadfast for ever and ever, done in faithfulness and uprightness. He provided redemption for his people; he ordained his covenant forever—holy and awesome is his name.

> Psalm 111:2–9

God is Here to Help

God is gently, lovingly, calling our names and inviting us to venture toward him, inviting us not to be afraid. He is not going to hurt us.

If your need right now is to overcome a difficult situation such as making it through the pain and anxiety of divorce, it's unlikely you can tap into God's overcoming power if you aren't convinced he is for you and not against you. If your overcoming need is to have the strength and wisdom to deal with your kids, who have turned their backs on God and on the family, that overcoming power has to be viewed as part of your family inheritance from the God who cares even more for your children than you do. If your overcoming need has to do with the devastation that comes from a cancer diagnosis or some other debilitating disease, you have to know that God's love for you will never leave you as you begin to walk a path you never expected to make your way down. His love guarantees you won't walk alone.

It's too good to be true, too big to be trusted, too foreign to be understood, yet he softly says, "I love you, I'm not going to hurt you. I love you."

MARILYN MEBERG

*B*ecause we live in a fallen world, we will experience negatives in our lives. Heartache and disappointment will come our way. We experience "stuff" we don't deserve, don't want, and can't send back. It's ours. But thanks be to God, nothing happens in this world that he doesn't know about and that he can't handle.

Regardless of the hurts you experience in life, you know someone who has the power to take those negatives and turn them into positives. You know someone whose holy powers aren't hindered by the crowd, by anyone's hidden agenda, by fear, by doubt, by whining, by complaining, or by other people's opinions. Nothing can negate Jesus Christ's power to bring healing and peace.

THELMA WELLS

Meditations on
God is Here to Help

As Jesus approached the town gate, a dead person was being carried out—the only son of his mother, and she was a widow. And a large crowd from the town was with her. When the Lord saw her, his heart went out to her and he said, "Don't cry." Then he went up and touched the coffin, and those carrying it stood still. He said, "Young man, I say to you, get up!" The dead man sat up and began to talk, and Jesus gave him back to his mother. They were all filled with awe and praised God. "A great prophet has appeared among us," they said. "God has come to help his people."

⥌ Luke 7:12–16

We know that in all things God works for the good of those who love him, who have been called according to his purpose.

⥌ Romans 8:28

God Is Good

Although I resonate with David's questions and fears and pleas in the first two-thirds of Psalm 13, I rest in his final two verses: "But I trust in your unfailing love; my heart rejoices in your salvation. I will sing to the LORD, for he has been good to me."

Until this point in his psalm, David poured out everything in his soul to God—and all he found there was sorrow, fear, despair, and anguish. But then it was as if he suddenly realized that no hope was to be found in his shriveled little heart. If hope was to be located, it would have to be sought outside of himself. And that was when he remembered: "He has been good to me." Not life has been good to me, or I have been good to me, or my friends have been good to me. Rather, *he* has been good to me. And that changed everything.

Only when we remember that God has been good to us can we turn from our fears and place our hope in him. He doesn't mind that we pour out our hearts to him; yet when they're empty, he wants us to come to him and be filled.

DAVE AND JAN DRAVECKY

God is so good,
God is so good,
God is so good,
He's so good to me!

He cares for me,
He cares for me,
He cares for me,
He's so good to me!

I love Him so,
I love Him so,
I love Him so,
He's so good to me!

I praise His Name,
I praise His Name,
I praise His Name,
He's so good to me!

TRADITIONAL

Meditations on
God Is Good

Who shall separate us from the love of Christ? Shall trouble or hardship or persecution or famine or nakedness or danger or sword? ... No, in all these things we are more than conquerors through him who loved us.

   Romans 8:35, 37

Grace and peace be yours in abundance through the knowledge of God and of Jesus our Lord. His divine power has given us everything we need for life and godliness through our knowledge of him who called us by his own glory and goodness. Through these he has given us his very great and precious promises, so that through them you may participate in the divine nature.

   2 Peter 1:2–4

God's Arms Hold Us

$\mathcal{M}$ost of us were taught rules as children. We started out believing life would be fair to us if we followed the rules. So we try to do well, to be "good." Then we, or someone we love, falls through the cracks. We experience some of life's exceptions, and we don't like it one bit. When things go wrong, we wonder, *Why? What about the rules?* And we exclaim, "This just isn't fair!"

God never said life would be fair. Life on this earth doesn't always play out according to rigid rules. Remember, God has been creating exceptions to the rules since time began. I, for one, am glad he doesn't treat me according to "the rules." Where would I be if I got what my sin really deserves?

We all need a way to survive our losses, to live with life's exceptions, to celebrate our joys in spite of our sorrows. We do that by grace, by remembering that God is never taken by surprise. His exceptions were built in before the dawn of time. So when you or the people you love fall through the cracks, you are going to fall right into his arms of grace. Hang in there!

BARBARA JOHNSON

There are many persons who, because of physical illness or emotional difficulties, feel at times they simply can't muster the energy to will themselves into a more positive, cheer-producing attitude. But no matter what frailties or infirmities arise to challenge you, remember that the love of God has no limits, no boundaries, and no prejudices. No matter who you are, where you are, or where you've been, he loves you. He holds you; he carries you; he remains with you at all times whether or not you feel him beside you in the Valley of the Shadow.

In the words of Hannah Whitall Smith, "Put together all the tenderest love you know, the deepest you have ever felt and the strongest that has ever been poured out upon you, and heap upon it all the love of all the loving human hearts in the world, and then multiply it by infinity, and you will begin, perhaps, to have some faint glimpse of the love God has for you."

MARILYN MEBERG

Meditations on God's Arms Hold Us

The eternal God is your refuge, and underneath are the everlasting arms.

❧ Deuteronomy 33:27

The Lord tends his flock like a shepherd: He gathers the lambs in his arms and carries them close to his heart; he gently leads those that have young.

❧ Isaiah 40:11

As a father has compassion on his children, so the Lord has compassion on those who fear him; for he knows how we are formed, he remembers that we are dust.

❧ Psalm 103:13–14

God Gives Us Courage

❦

*W*hen I was a young minister's wife and new mother, I suffered from a serious case of low self-image and overcautiousness. It was very difficult for me to speak to a group of more than seven or eight ladies. When asked to speak, I would often hide behind my husband's ministerial cloak and say that he was the speaker and I was his "helpmeet."

While attending a church school conference, God used Dr. Henry Brandt, a Christian psychologist, to minister his truth to me. Dr. Brandt used 2 Timothy 1:7 as his text; and that day, for the first time, I began to realize that my fears and anxieties were self-imposed. God's choice for me was to have power, love and self-discipline.

Over a period of weeks, and then months, it began to be obvious that God was changing me.

Now, many years later, I can say, "Thank you, Lord" for what he has done in me. I would not want to go back to the former Beverly for anything in the world—and the greatest thing is that God is not finished with me yet!

BEVERLY LAHAYE

*T*here resides in the heart of every believer little pockets of fear. For some of us it's cowardice. For others, it's timidity. Although we know the Savior gives courage and power, sometimes we feel safer in our little pocket than in his big provision. So we cower inside, afraid to be bold. We permit our human frailty to stand in the way of his strength.

Amazingly though, God has grace for this kind of behavior. He understands our weaknesses. Just because [my friend] spoke up and I didn't, that doesn't mean he likes her better than he does me. I take such comfort in that because even in my most unbecoming, inept, self-loathing moments, God still loves me with all his heart. When my weakness prevails rather than his strength, he doesn't condemn me. He doesn't compare me to [my friends]. Now when I come face-to-face with my less-than-perfect behavior, instead of condemning or comparing, I'm learning to lean on him and pray, "Lord, make me more like you. When I want to retreat, give me your courage." He longs to and he does.

LUCI SWINDOLL

Meditations on
God Gives Us Courage

Be strong and courageous. Do not be terrified; do not be discouraged, for the LORD your God will be with you wherever you go.

        ❧ Joshua 1:9

God did not give us a spirit of timidity, but a spirit of power, of love and of self-discipline.

        ❧ 2 Timothy 1:7

The LORD is my light and my salvation— whom shall I fear? The LORD is the stronghold of my life—of whom shall I be afraid? ... Wait for the LORD; be strong and take heart and wait for the LORD.

        ❧ Psalm 27:1, 14

The Past, the Present, the Future

How briskly the hours and days speed by! What a tragedy that most of us spend fifty-nine minutes of every hour living in the past. We waste so much time nursing regrets over lost jobs or soured relationships; we harbor shame for things poorly done. But dwelling on what cannot be changed will only steal our precious joy today.

To face a titanic hour with cool calm is grace. To speak words of wisdom when the boat is sinking is grace. And to swim in deep waters of adversity rather than drown in despair is grace. When things go slow, go bad, go sour, or go away, it's time to unwrap the life preserver of God's love and stay afloat on the boundless ocean of his grace.

But don't wait for catastrophe before you unwrap grace. Embrace it today. Remember, friend, the past is gone. The future is unknown. There is only one minute in which you are alive. This minute! Right here, right now.

BARBARA JOHNSON

*A*s we look into the unknown future, with no clear path before us, we may become fearful. But God has provided for our future. Paul wrote, "and my God will meet all your needs according to his glorious riches in Christ Jesus" (Philippians 4:19). It does not say "perhaps he will provide," or "he is able to," but he "will" provide. God is our hope for the future.

We can thank him for the past and have confidence in him for the future. Yet sometimes we find it difficult to trust him for the needs of today. But we must remember he is willing to do the same for us today as he did in the past and will do in the future. He is the great "I am" of today, the all-sufficient One for this very moment.

Sometimes he takes us out of situations, problems or needs; other times he takes us through them. Regardless of the way he works in our lives, we can trust him as our ever-present guide for today.

 MILLIE STAMM

Meditations on the Past, the Present, the Future

*K*now also that wisdom is sweet to
your soul; if you find it, there is a
future hope for you, and your hope
will not be cut off.

      Proverbs 24:14

*T*he LORD watches over you—the
LORD is your shade at your right
hand; the sun will not harm you by
day, nor the moon by night. The
LORD will keep you from all harm—
he will watch over your life; the LORD
will watch over your coming and
going both now and forevermore.

      Psalm 121:5–8

*A*s for God, his way is perfect; the
word of the LORD is flawless. He is a
shield for all who take refuge in him.

      Psalm 18:30

The God of Love Is in Charge

✿

*W*hen I fell—when I had no more physical or emotional strength left—I was surprised to find that I fell straight into the hands of God. That shocked me. How could this be? I wasn't manipulating circumstances anymore. I wasn't making anything happen. It had to be God who was now making things happen. It had to be God who started bringing people into my life, people who would help me to heal. What a relief to finally realize that it wasn't Jan Dravecky who was in charge, but God!

What suffering and persecution and pain and difficulties do is not so much *make* us weak, as show us we *are* weak. Without them, we can deceive ourselves into believing we're prizefighters. With them, we're reminded that we're not constructed to function on our own power. The trick is to allow suffering to be used as a tool to help us depend on God and not upon ourselves.

JAN DRAVECKY

I am thankful that even when I don't understand the Lord or his ways (just like I don't understand the Internet), I can still depend on him by faith. When computers, calendars, and clocks seem to get the best of me and my time, I rely on the One who never changes. I figure God put me on earth to accomplish a certain number of things (right now I'm so far behind, I'll never die), but God is my hiding place from tyranny of the urgent. Because of his grace, I can luxuriate in the knowledge that all is well—even when the bits and bytes of my life look like scrambled gobbledygook.

Like the Internet superhighway, we have access to grace at any time of day or night. This grace connects us with God himself and with people worldwide who have signed on to follow him. By faith we hyperlink to the wisdom we need to live by his kingdom principles.

What is it you need today? Remember that you have immediate access to God's Riches At Christ's Expense (GRACE). It's all right there, waiting for you to dial in. Jesus said, "God's kingdom is within you." Click on that!

BARBARA JOHNSON

Meditations on the God of Love Is in Charge

If the LORD delights in a man's way, he makes his steps firm; though he stumble, he will not fall, for the LORD upholds him with his hand.

     🌿 Psalm 37:23–24

I heard what sounded like a great multitude, like the roar of rushing waters and like loud peals of thunder, shouting: "Hallelujah! For our Lord God Almighty reigns. Let us rejoice and be glad and give him glory! For the wedding of the Lamb has come, and his bride has made herself ready."

     🌿 Revelation 19:6–7

How beautiful on the mountains are the feet of those who bring good news, who proclaim peace, who bring good tidings, who proclaim salvation, who say to Zion, "Your God reigns!" Listen! Your watchmen lift up their voices; together they shout for joy. When the LORD returns to Zion, they will see it with their own eyes.

     🌿 Isaiah 52:7–8

Ordinary Yet Unique

Sometimes we have the mistaken idea that God loves and blesses us more if we look, live, or behave a certain way. If our lives are tidier, he's happier. If we are "successful" in the world's eyes, he's relieved. If we become cultured or erudite, he feels better about us. We assume God prefers designer clothes and custom homes. We presume he's pleased with fancy careers and technological advances. But in God's economy, grace doesn't work like that. God places *no* emphasis on externals. He looks at our hearts, and he blesses us from the inside out. His goodness is available to *all*.

God's grace is limitless. It's not dependent on anything we've done—or have. God gives us himself, in the person of Jesus Christ, and he does it whether we live in a New York City penthouse or under a thatched roof at the foot of a volcano. He loves us infinitely, with extravagant grace!

LUCI SWINDOLL

*A*ccording to my calculations, reality is this very second. You see, yesterday is only a memory, and tomorrow is merely a dream. Today is an illusion. That leaves this one second. Every day you have 86,400 seconds. But they come only one at a time. In your bank account of time, no balance is carried over until the next day. You use those seconds or lose them. There is no chance to reinvest.

Make your investment wisely by believing you deserve to be full of joy this very second. And you can be. Decide to be. Don't put it off until you finish your chores; instead, make tedious tasks a game. Compete with yourself. Reward yourself. Make work play.

Be curious about everything and everyone. You'll get tickled in the process!

Trust the heavenly Father of Goodness. Giggle at his artistic genius in the world. Always remember you're created unique—just like everyone else!

BARBARA JOHNSON

Meditations on Ordinary Yet Unique

*F*rom the beginning God chose you to be saved through the sanctifying work of the Spirit and through belief in the truth. He called you to this through our gospel, that you might share in the glory of our Lord Jesus Christ.

🌿 2 Thessalonians 2:13–14

I, the LORD, have called you in righteousness; I will take hold of your hand."

🌿 Isaiah 42:6

*I*f you belong to Christ, you are . . . heirs according to the promise.

🌿 Galatians 3:29

*J*esus said, "You do not belong to the world, but I have chosen you out of the world."

🌿 John 15:19

Rest in the Shadow
of the Almighty

❧

*W*ith all my years of traveling, I've slept in some strange places. My great comfort when I'm far away from home is that the Lord never sleeps but watches over me whether I'm in Bangkok, Britain, or Boise, Idaho.

I remember staying with an old lady in Bristol, England, who had forty-three cats. That night the gang made themselves comfortable on my bed, in my suitcase, and in my toilet bag. As I went to sleep I prayed, "Lord, please keep these beasts off me while I'm sleeping."

I woke up to find I was suffocating and realized there's a cat on my face!

I have lots of fun stories to tell and laugh about in the comfort of my own home. But every story is held together by the common thread of God's faithfulness through it all. He was my constant companion.

Is it ever hard for you to close your eyes at night? Do you worry about what tomorrow will hold or if you will be safe until morning? Psalm 121 makes it clear God never closes his eyes. He is always watching over you . . . even if you have fur in your mouth.

SHEILA WALSH

The other night I took care of my grandchildren. Six-year-old Shane woke up crying. He had been dreaming of goblins and other childhood terrors. After he quieted down, he showed me the well-worn Bible his grandfather had given him. Shane always keeps it under his pillow. As I left the room, he said, "You know, Grandma, when you sleep with your Bible, it's almost like sleeping with Jesus!" And he lay down like a little lamb and went to sleep. He was resting in the shadow of the Almighty. Later I found myself asking, "Is this where I'm resting today?"

Try reading Psalm 91 every day for the next month. Your life will be changed, as mine was, because this is a triumphant song of faith. In it we learn that God is our dwelling place. It's under his wings that we find refuge even in the midst of the universal evil that surrounds us.

We all face dangers and heartaches in life because we live in a lost and fallen world. But in the midst of these difficulties we can be absolutely confident that we are not left alone to deal with them. God's faithfulness is our constant shield.

HOPE MCDONALD

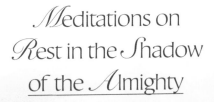

Meditations on Rest in the Shadow of the Almighty

I will lie down and sleep in peace, for you alone, O LORD, make me dwell in safety.

Psalm 4:8

I lift up my eyes to the hills—where does my help come from? My help comes from the LORD, the Maker of heaven and earth. He will not let your foot slip—he who watches over you will not slumber; indeed, he who watches over Israel will neither slumber nor sleep.

Psalm 121:1–4

He who dwells in the shelter of the Most High will rest in the shadow of the Almighty. I will say of the LORD, "He is my refuge and my fortress, my God, in whom I trust."

Psalm 91:1–2

106

The Great Provider

As a young Christian in college I was often on my knees asking the Lord to help with college fees and even incidentals—stockings, underwear, notebook paper and a warm scarf. The wonderful thing was that when I sought him in prayer, he answered!

The main building on our college campus was perched on a hill overlooking the Hudson River. The setting was beautiful. Maneuvering was more difficult. It was easy going when we walked down into the town but coming back was the struggle. I learned and quoted Psalm 34 on those walks up the hillside. I knew then, as I know now, that anyone—man, woman, young, old, rich, poor, black or white—can call on the Lord, and he will answer and meet the need.

If you have been going through a difficult period in your life, if you have been crushed by some unkind deed, or if you have lost a loved one and are feeling the pangs of loneliness, remember: "the LORD is close to the brokenhearted" (Psalm 34:18). Why not take refuge in him?

WANDA K. JONES

HOPE IN GOD'S LOVE

*M*y business was firmly established by 1984 when I resigned from the bank to be a full-time entrepreneur. Money was no object because I was making plenty of it—until 1986 when banks started failing. Within six weeks, I lost all my speaking contracts.

Outside banking I had no credibility, but I thought I was good enough to market myself fast enough to be on my feet in short order. Not! For one year, I did everything in my power to get work. Nothing worked! By now, money was running out and I was on a first-name basis with several bill collectors.

During that period, God led three of those creditors to extend grace to me. I did not deserve the goodness I received. It was granted though, in spite of me. Good times returned. Cash flowed again. I paid my bills and began to get on my feet. Everything I thought I had lost during that down time has been regained, and more.

My creditors' grace is only a flicker of the splendor of God's grace toward each of us. It's yours, my friend. Receive it.

THELMA WELLS

Meditations on the Great Provider

The LORD *is gracious and compassionate. He provides food for those who fear him; he remembers his covenant forever.*

> ❧ Psalm 111:4–5

Command those who are rich in this present world not to be arrogant nor to put their hope in wealth, which is so uncertain, but to put their hope in God, who richly provides us with everything for our enjoyment.

> ❧ 1 Timothy 6:17

Jesus said, "Ask and it will be given to you; seek and you will find; knock and the door will be opened to you."

> ❧ Matthew 7:7

The Waiting Arms of God

❧

*W*hen I finally decided to turn my back and run away from God, he let me walk to the edge. He let me walk to a place where I realized that no one loved me as he did. Just as my mother would not have let me really run away, God wouldn't either. I am his child; but in his great wisdom, he let me realize that nowhere else in the whole wide world, nowhere in all creation, can I go from his presence. He wouldn't let me go.

What a wonderful and humbling realization!

All this time I thought I was holding on to God, grasping with all my earthly might not to let go. And that is precisely why God told me to let go. He knew that when I finally loosened my grip, I would realize he was holding me fast.

God's Word and his promises began to sink in. I realized, *I really do believe this!* And for the first time in months, I felt a glimmering of hope.

JAN DRAVECKY

*W*hen I was visiting a dear friend, she asked me to read a card she'd received from her son. He had gone through a difficult time and had sent this card to let his parents know that he was fine, that his trust was still in the Lord. The message included the "Footprints" poem. I'd read it before but now was reminded again of the tender compassion of God toward a weary pilgrim.

God understands that we are not strong all the time. Sometimes all we can do is rest in his arms as he takes us the next few miles. Things happen to us that break our hearts; our legs may buckle under us. But we are not left lying by the side of the road like a failed runner counted out of the race. When our trust is in Christ and our hearts are committed to our journey home, the One who walks beside us bends and gently picks us up and carries us for a while.

SHEILA WALSH

Meditations on the Waiting Arms of God

I will set out and go back to my father and say to him: Father, I have sinned against heaven and against you. I am no longer worthy to be called your son; make me like one of your hired men." So he got up and went to his father. But while he was still a long way off, his father saw him and was filled with compassion for him; he ran to his son, threw his arms around him and kissed him.

  ❧ Luke 15:18–20

The LORD reached down from on high and took hold of me; he drew me out of deep waters. . . . He brought me out into a spacious place; he rescued me because he delighted in me.

  ❧ Psalm 18:16, 19

Jesus said, "Come to me, all you who are weary and burdened, and I will give you rest."

  ❧ Matthew 11:28

God Loves No Matter What

❧

*I*s anyone good enough for God? No one is! Because if our behavior doesn't condemn us, then our thought life does. God knows that, looks beyond our imperfect performance, and loves and receives us anyway. Jesus made that kind of grace possible on the cross by dying for the sin that inspires bad performances. It really is that simple.

When we admit that our performance will never measure up to God's standard, then we can quit trying to make ourselves good enough and concentrate instead on having a *relationship* with him. Everything, absolutely everything—from my tendency to be selfish to why the snails won't leave my potted plants alone—is acceptable to talk to him about.

A relationship based on love for who I am and grace in spite of what I do causes me to melt in gratitude, humility, and tenderness. When I know that God looks beyond my performance to the woman he loves, I can't but sink into his embrace, recognizing yet again that it is this for which I thirst.

MARILYN MEBERG

Think of your own life. Stop for a moment and reflect on any situation where it seemed as if you were on your own, that it was hopeless, that you were forgotten. Remember how you could never have anticipated God showing up, but he did, with flying colors—even if it seemed like he left you dangling just a little too long for comfort!

I don't know what the circumstances of your life are right now, or how fast you feel you're falling, or whether you're frozen on the bar, afraid to let go and grab hold of God's hands. What I can tell you is that he is here, right now, and he won't let you go. He will catch you in midair. The net of his faithful love will cushion you when you free-fall.

SHEILA WALSH

Meditations on God Loves No Matter What

I am always with you, LORD; you hold me by my right hand.

   ❧ Psalm 73:23

*I*n your unfailing love you will lead the people you have redeemed. In your strength you will guide them to your holy dwelling.

   ❧ Exodus 15:13

*T*he eyes of the LORD are on those who fear him, on those whose hope is in his unfailing love.

   ❧ Psalm 33:18

*F*rom everlasting to everlasting the LORD's love is with those who fear him, and his righteousness with their children's children.

   ❧ Psalm 103:17

Talking to God

*H*ave you ever attempted to get in touch with God and found yourself doubting his ability to help you? Do you find yourself carrying around things you should tell God about instead? Do you feel ashamed to talk to God? Do you find yourself seeking other people's opinions rather than relying on God's guidance? Do you think you have to use a certain posture or language to get God's attention? Do you think you've done something so awful you can't tell God?

If your answer is "yes" to any of those questions, you're creating unnecessary interference between you and God. It doesn't matter what time of day or night it is; what day of the week it is; who else is talking to him; or what the problem is. He is always available to listen and to help us without static or interference. His omnipotence has blocked out anything and everything that would keep him from hearing and answering us.

THELMA WELLS

*T*o pray is a supernatural way of getting to know a supernatural God. When we pray, God makes us his partners! He chooses us to become part of his ministry here on earth.

When Jesus inquires, "May I help you?" he wants us to respond in childlike trust. He wants us to ask. Sometimes he answers in a miraculous way, but most of the time he simply opens our spiritual eyes and shows us what we can do to bring about the answer. Then he gives us the ability to do it.

To believe is to give God the right to answer our prayer in the way he sees best. Remember, Jesus never gave a sermon on unanswered prayer because, from his viewpoint, all prayers are answered. When we learn to believe God, we find our attention is no longer on our mountain. It becomes focused instead on Jesus, who alone is worthy of our trust.

HOPE MACDONALD

Meditations on Talking to God

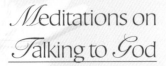

Jesus said, "Therefore I tell you, whatever you ask for in prayer, believe that you have received it, and it will be yours."

    Mark 11:24

I watch in hope for the LORD, I wait for God my Savior; my God will hear me.

    Micah 7:7

Dear friends, if our hearts do not condemn us, we have confidence before God and receive from him anything we ask, because we obey his commands and do what pleases him.

    1 John 3:21–22

Cast your cares on the LORD and he will sustain you; he will never let the righteous fall.

    Psalm 55:22

Is any one of you in trouble? He should pray. Is anyone happy? Let him sing songs of praise. Is any one of you sick? He should call the elders of the church to pray over him and anoint him with oil in the name of the Lord. And the prayer offered in faith will make the sick person well; the Lord will raise him up. If he has sinned, he will be forgiven. Therefore confess your sins to each other and pray for each other so that you may be healed. The prayer of a righteous man is powerful and effective.

James 5:13–16

Hope
to Share

Hope to Pass On

❧

*M*y mother had a way of making Scripture very practical, and it proved life-changing. For example, she held tremendous hope for all three of her children, and her hope came straight from Scripture: "A man's gift maketh room for him, and bringeth him before great men (Proverbs 18:16 KJV). She wrote that verse on a three-by-five card and taped it above her kitchen sink. "I'm claiming this for my three children," she told my brother one day. While Babe and Orville and I fought over baseballs, household chores, and who ate the last Popsicle, Mother was praying about our futures. She was believing God's promise that our various gifts would give us opportunities to minister to people "of importance," as the *Living Bible* puts it. Her hope for that outcome wasn't in her children (at the moment, we were giving her little hope); her hope was in God's faithfulness to his Word.

■ LUCI SWINDOLL

*C*hristian women who have had the heart to seek not their own have had an enormous impact on the world. If love had not motivated women who are a part of our spiritual heritage to seek not their own, there would have been no missions as we know them today, prison reform would still be in the dark ages, nursing would be undeveloped, and orphans would still roam the streets begging for food. This is some sorority! Join the sorority of sisters whose expansive souls, through deeds of loving-kindness, have brought Christ and belonging to the most hopeless and helpless "element." Why not experience Kenya at sixty? Why not fill your house with children when you are seventy? A woman expands her heart to God's dimensions may find life taking on a more adventurous tone as the calendar marches through her years.

VALERIE BELL

Meditations on Hope to Pass On

Do not forget to do good and to share with others, for with such sacrifices God is pleased.

    Hebrews 13:16

Let us not give up meeting together, as some are in the habit of doing, but let us encourage one another—and all the more as you see the Day approaching.

    Hebrews 10:25

Always be prepared to give an answer to everyone who asks you to give the reason for the hope that you have.

    1 Peter 3:15

Encourage one another and build each other up, just as in fact you are doing.

    1 Thessalonians 5:11

Sharing God's Grace

I used to be more concerned with being "inspirational" than with being real, but I now sense that people in pain need to know that they are not alone in their struggles; we need each other to be real. I am not advocating a coast-to-coast spiritual pity party, far from it. Rather, I suggest that as we receive the help and comfort of Christ, we in turn take a risk and extend that same hope and comfort to others. This is not a time to hide behind walls and put on a brave face; this is a time to stand in the light with our wounds and our flaws. Having taken that risk, we can encourage others to risk and come out of the shadows, find healing and find comfort in Christ. Those who reach out, who risk being known, will have the privilege of sharing the grace and mercy of God with others.

SHEILA WALSH

I gather grace-filled encouragement from readers all over the country in the form of inspirational quotes and jokes. I enjoy cutting them out and pasting them together on the pages of my newsletter, *The Love Line*. My readers are blessed, they send me more "grace notes" to share, and God's grace just increases, like compounding interest. "I am too blessed to be stressed," wrote one reader. Another said, "I enjoy the cherries, and spit the pits!" These people are exceptions to the way life beats us up. They choose to celebrate the gift of grace.

Friend, if your life is bumpy these days, grab the grace to be real and to be as odd as you really are. Make pleasing designs with the bumps of life rather than trying to get rid of them. Remember that grace is like peanut butter: you can't spread it around without getting some on yourself!

BARBARA JOHNSON

Meditations on Sharing God's Grace

We have different gifts, according to the grace given us . . . if it is encouraging, let him encourage; if it is contributing to the needs of others, let him give generously; if it is leadership, let him govern diligently; if it is showing mercy, let him do it cheerfully.

∙ Romans 12:6, 8

God is able to make all grace abound to you, so that in all things at all times, having all that you need, you will abound in every good work.

∙ 2 Corinthians 9:8

Make sure that nobody pays back wrong for wrong, but always try to be kind to each other and to everyone else.

∙ 1 Thessalonians 5:15

Transforming Attitudes

❧

*J*esus Christ never taught that one person should tell another what to do, where to go, how to live. In fact, he reserved his harshest comments for those who tried. Jesus said, "Follow me." He never instructed us to follow each other's rules. He never gave anyone control over another. His desire is that his Word and his Spirit be our guides for life. Being a follower of Jesus Christ means becoming more and more like him . . . letting his Spirit transform us into all we were created to be. That happens, dear friend, from the inside out.

Unfortunately, there will always be people in the world ready to pounce on anything that smacks of grace and freedom. They'll be standing in the wings of your life, waiting to make their entrance with demands, curfews, criticism, and rules. They're always close at hand, wanting to squelch the passion and pleasure of knowing the Savior. Don't let them. And, with all the love in the world, let me say: Don't be one! As a follower of Christ you have the unique opportunity every day to demonstrate and celebrate his grace.

LUCI SWINDOLL

*O*ne of my favorite pastoral calls with my father was to Mr. and Mrs. Wheeler's farm. Mrs. Wheeler was the most pleasant, jolly and "laughy" lady I've ever known. It wasn't that Mrs. Wheeler couldn't think of any sad thought to consider. I learned some years later that the Wheelers's only child had died of rheumatic fever at the age of six. Apparently, they had made a conscious choice about how they would cope with their loss. They chose "glad" over "sad," and they and those around them were the richer as a result of that choice.

We are all capable of increasing our state of cheerfulness. Being of good cheer is an attitude of the mind made possible by God's enabling power within us. As we remember that Christ, our firm foundation, never moves or wavers, we can, then, in partnership with him, make choices about our habits of mind that produce attitudes of cheer.

Remember, Jesus is watching you, guarding your mind, encouraging you to develop the habit of cheerfulness.

MARILYN MEBERG

Meditations on Transforming Attitudes

Jesus said, "I have told you these things, so that in me you may have peace. In this world you will have trouble. But take heart! I have overcome the world."

&❧ John 16:33

May our Lord Jesus Christ himself and God our Father, who loved us and by his grace gave us eternal encouragement and good hope, encourage your hearts and strengthen you in every good deed and word.

&❧ 2 Thessalonians 2:16–17

I pray that out of his glorious riches he may strengthen you with power through his Spirit in your inner being, so that Christ may dwell in your hearts through faith. And I pray that you, being rooted and established in love, may have power, together with all the saints, to grasp how wide and long and high and deep is the love of Christ.

&❧ Ephesians 3:16–18

Share the
Hope of Heaven

I don't know exactly how my thirteen-year-old daughter, Jessica, came to grasp the reality of heaven, but she certainly did. Through her three-and-one-half year struggle with cancer—the horrible chemotherapy, the final weakening stage—her confidence in what lay ahead for her never wavered. I was amazed by how real heaven was to her. I was inspired by her complete peace. I found encouragement in her lack of fear or dread. Our hope, our comfort, and our strength for grieving were immeasurably enhanced by the powerful simplicity of her faith.

I will never forget our last evening with her. She was obviously near death and leaned across my chest. "I'm ready to go now, Daddy," she said.

"Do you mean go to heaven?"

"Yes, Daddy, I'm ready to go over there."

We prayed together one last time, and, surrounded by her family, Jessica slipped peacefully into a coma. A few hours later, God gently took her home.

 RON EGGERT

*C*ultivate, then, your hope, dearly beloved. Make it to shine so plainly in you that your minister may hear of your hopefulness and joy, cause observers to take note of it because you speak of heaven and act as though you really expected to go there. Make the world know that you have a hope of heaven . . . that you are a believer in eternal glory and that you hope to be where Jesus is.

CHARLES HADDON SPURGEON

Meditations for Sharing the Hope of Heaven

*S*o that, having been justified by his grace, we might become heirs having the hope of eternal life.

❧ Titus 3:7

*W*e do not lose heart. Though outwardly we are wasting away, yet inwardly we are being renewed day by day. For our light and momentary troubles are achieving for us an eternal glory that far outweighs them all. So we fix our eyes not on what is seen, but on what is unseen. For what is seen is temporary, but what is unseen is eternal.

❧ 2 Corinthians 4:16–18

Shine in God's Light

My friend Thelma is a light-bearer of the brightest kind. When Thelma has faced difficult days, times when the Prince of Darkness has tried to trip her up, she has reached even deeper into her arsenal of God's light-giving truth. Thelma is a solar light who faithfully stores light while it is day. I have benefited from seeing the commitment in her life, for while Thelma is capable of being feisty, what you see is faithful because of God's grace aglow in her soul. You shine, girlfriend!

What does it take to be a solar-powered sister? A relationship with Christ, a dedication to his Word, and God's brilliant grace. If you need greater clarification in your life, if you're uncertain what next step you should take, if you long to make a difference in your world, then invite Christ to bring the light of his life into your darkened understanding. If you've done that and still feel as if you're stumbling around, then redouble your efforts to be in his light-bearing Word. Gather up his truth, store it in your heart, and then shine like crazy.

PATSY CLAIRMONT

*W*ith the world living in so much emotional and spiritual darkness, you'd think everybody would gravitate toward light. But they don't. Often, people don't even know they're groping and fretting in the dark. They wander around without the peace, safety, and comfort that light brings.

God is teaching us to unwrap, appreciate, enjoy, share, and celebrate the gifts of his grace. It is my hope that you will open your heart to him and see all the ways God is illuminating your path with grace. Right in your own household, backyard, neighborhood, workplace . . . there is grace in abundance.

When we live in the light we see it, recognize it for what it is, thank God for it, and eagerly pass it on to somebody else. Jesus told us he is the light of the world, and whoever follows him will never walk in darkness, but will have the light of life. What a gift—that we will not only walk in light but we will reflect his light. I want you to shine where you are. It's possible, because everyone who follows Jesus is his light.

LUCI SWINDOLL

Meditations on Shine in God's Light

Come, . . . let us walk in the light of the LORD.

    ❧ Isaiah 2:5

Jesus said, "Let your light shine before men, that they may see your good deeds and praise your Father in heaven."

    ❧ Matthew 5:16

You are a chosen people, a royal priesthood, a holy nation, a people belonging to God, that you may declare the praises of him who called you out of darkness into his wonderful light.

    ❧ 1 Peter 2:9

Share the Good News

❦

I'm grateful that our hope in Christ goes far beyond what we see in a mirror. Whew! Otherwise we would become people of despair. I mean, do you watch the evening news? Yikes! Now there's a scary mirror. Talk about a world full of distortions and contortions, in which humankind often appears wrenched and wretched: children shooting children, rampant brutality, pervasive dishonesty, war atrocities, killer storms, moral decay, dismal predictions. . . . Hey, would somebody send out for popcorn? I'm starting to feel depressed!

But here's the best news from the Good News: Jesus eliminated distortions through the contortion of the cross. His twisted and broken body offered as a sacrifice for all has given us new reflective hope. Instead of seeing ourselves through our hopeless human condition, we have been given a divine perspective with an everlasting future. Jesus breaks the cords that bind us; he actually sets captives free. Now that's outrageous! Oh, I love a happy ending.

PATSY CLAIRMONT

At Christmas I wanted to make a card for my friend to commemorate the season in a unique and special way. She had just returned from a mission trip to Russia, so I drew a Russian Orthodox church on the front of a card. Under it I planned to write "Merry Christmas" in Russian. But I could not find out how to say it in that language.

Instead I simply found a short Russian word followed by a long one (looked like Merry Christmas to me!) and used them. The words I chose actually meant "One-Way Street." As I printed them, it hit me: "One-Way Street" was a very appropriate way to say Merry Christmas! So, I added this note to the card:

"Actually, I wanted this to say Merry Christmas in Russian, but I couldn't find it. So it says One-Way Street, which is sort of the same thing when you think about it. The birth of Christ is the One Way to peace, hope, joy, laughter . . . all that Christmas means. May Christmas be all of that and more to you, dearest Mary—a one-way street to happiness."

LUCI SWINDOLL

Meditations to Share the Good News

Do not be ashamed to testify about our Lord.... But join with me in suffering for the gospel, by the power of God, who has saved us and called us to a holy life—not because of anything we have done but because of his own purpose and grace.

2 Timothy 1:8–9

The angel said to [the shepherds], "Do not be afraid. I bring you good news of great joy that will be for all the people. Today in the town of David a Savior has been born to you; he is Christ the Lord."

Luke 2:10–11

The Spirit of the Sovereign LORD is on me, because the LORD has anointed me to preach good news to the poor.

Isaiah 61:1

Cheerful,
Thankful Living

❧

I don't usually respond to formulas for this and that; they feel a bit too tidy. But I have developed one for cheerful thinking I'd like to toss your way for your consideration. To begin with, I love to laugh. I believe a giggle is always loitering about even in the most devastating of circumstances. I make a point of shuffling through the rubble in search of that giggle.

This isn't denial. I need to feel and express my pain. But I also need to find the light side—and there is *always* a light side! I've noticed that when I laugh about some minor part of a problem or controversy or worry the whole situation suddenly seems much less negative to me. After a good laugh, I can then rethink my circumstances. As a result, that which was threatening may now seem less threatening.

MARILYN MEBERG

I'm learning to stop for thankful moments. It's become a daily discipline of mine since I found that I was getting overwhelmed by all the daily stuff that "has to get done." Some of the feelings and fears I had before I was hospitalized for clinical depression were niggling at me again, buzzing around me like persistent house flies. I've learned enough about what makes me tick to pay attention when I feel myself sinking. So I'm learning to stop intentionally throughout every day and lift my heart and soul to heaven and say, "Thank you!"

Giving thanks does wonder for my soul. It refocuses me on what's really important. We can dwell every day on the things that are not working and let them drag us down, or we can thank God for the simple gifts of grace he gives us every day if we have a heart to see them.

SHEILA WALSH

Meditations for Cheerful, Thankful Living

I saw the Lord always before me. Because he is at my right hand, I will not be shaken. Therefore my heart is glad and my tongue rejoices; my body also will live in hope.

🌿 Acts 2:25–26

God has brought me laughter. . . .

🌿 Genesis 21:6

You are my God, and I will give you thanks; you are my God and I will exalt you.

🌿 Psalm 118:28

Be joyful always; pray continually; give thanks in all circumstances, for this is God's will for you in Christ Jesus.

🌿 1 Thessalonians 5:16–18

Exercising Grace

❧

*M*y friend realized that various containers were a metaphor for herself; she was an empty vessel waiting to be filled. She was thirsty for grace. Then she considered that each pitcher in her home was equipped with a pour spout. God seemed to be telling her that he wanted her to pour out this fullness into the lives of others. She wondered how effective she had been at doing that.

Surely, God's intention is that we overflow when he fills us to the brim! And it doesn't take a monumental feat to exercise grace toward others. It can be as simple as letting someone ahead of you in line. Grace always remembers that it's not your job to get people to like you, it's your job to like people.

Grace is all around and within you, just like my friend's empty vessels. So stand still awhile, your soul ajar. Notice grace. Appreciate it. As it flows into your open soul, drink deeply. And then from your fullness in Christ, pour out his grace on others.

BARBARA JOHNSON

I was aware of the woman before she reached me in line. She looked angry and troubled.

"I heard the title of your new book on the radio," she said. "I wanted to slap you! My life is falling apart. My husband left me. I have two kids who need me. I'm struggling to make it through one more day, and you write some nice little Christian book called *Life Is Tough But God Is Faithful!*"

I felt such empathy for her. I took her in my arms and held her as she wept.

"I am so sorry," I said.

That night, I thought back to the days before my life fell apart. I imagined my encounter then with a woman in that kind of pain. I realized that all I would have seen was someone attacking me. I would have missed the aching soul behind the words. Since those dark days in my own life, I have learned that when, at your lowest moment, you are gifted with grace and acceptance, you are given fresh grace for others, too.

Sheila Walsh

Meditations on Exercising Grace

Share with God's people who are in need. Practice hospitality.

    🔖 Romans 12:13

I commit you to God and to the word of his grace, which can build you up and give you an inheritance among all those who are sanctified.

    🔖 Acts 20:32

Carry each other's burdens, and in this way you will fulfill the law of Christ.

    🔖 Galatians 6:2

Just as you excel in everything—in faith, in speech, in knowledge, in complete earnestness and in your love for us—see that you also excel in this grace of giving.

    🔖 2 Corinthians 8:7

Acceptance
Through God's Grace

❧

*I*n Jesus' day, many people believed sickness was a result of sin in a person's life. Religious people especially shied away from cripples or lepers, thinking they had brought misfortune on themselves. Whether or not that was true didn't matter to Jesus. He healed as many as called on him. He forgave them, too.

We all need grace at its best! Grace is simply knowing all about someone and loving them just the same. Jesus extends that grace to us every moment—and his Spirit in us enables us to graciously overlook the unbecoming, understand the unconventional, tolerate the unpleasant, overcome the unexpected, and outlast the unbearable in ourselves and other people.

Grace is God's reality check in a phony-baloney world. When we no longer deny that we're ordinary, we don't need to judge anyone. We offer grace to all. Remember, friends, your arms are the only ones God has to hug other people.

BARBARA JOHNSON

*W*hen I served on the HIV (He Intends Victory) board, three of the members, two men and a woman, were HIV positive. One of the men had contracted the virus through homosexual relations with an infected partner. The other man was hemophiliac and got the virus in a blood transfusion before the nation's blood supply was as carefully monitored as it is now. The woman got it through an unprotected promiscuous lifestyle.

It became clear to me as I served beside these brothers and sister in Christ that how they got the disease was irrelevant. God's grace is sufficient for all situations. If we don't believe that, then we render Calvary limited in its power to redeem. Every man, woman, and child who walks this earth is indelibly imprinted with the image of God. We can hold up the standard of a righteous way of life, but we have to leave room for those who are suffering to lay their head on our breast. As God's children we have a divine mandate to extend grace to those in need.

SHEILA WALSH

Meditations on Accepting Others Through God's Grace

Accept one another, then, just as Christ accepted you, in order to bring praise to God.

> Romans 15:7

There is neither Jew nor Greek, slave nor free, male nor female, for you are all one in Christ Jesus.

> Galatians 3:28

The tongue that brings healing is a tree of life.

> Proverbs 15:4

Deep-rooted Hope

❧

*O*ur experience has taught Jan and me that God keeps his promises. He is faithful to his Word and it is that Word that he uses to renew us. When our emotions are out of control and we can't feel him or sense him, that is the time we need to rely on the firm foundation of God's Word. His Word sustains us.

A verse in the Psalms captures the heart of our discovery. Psalm 119:92 says, "If your law had not been my delight, I would have perished in my affliction." We can both say a hearty "amen!" to that. But because we have allowed God's Word to take root in the soil of our souls, we can see it bearing fruit. And the great thing about being born again of imperishable seed is that your flower never falls and your grass never withers.

DAVE AND JAN DRAVECKY

*W*hen I was working on my album, "Hope," it was very important to me that every song contained this rich truth that God is weaving through the tapestry of my own life. I wanted my listeners to feel like I was sitting down with them, one at a time, hand in hand, and singing to them about the hope that does not disappoint. When you've been in a dark place and have lost hope, and into that solitary cell the Lamb of God has come to sit and weep with you, and then carried you out, you long to share that hope with others. Hope is no longer just in my head; it's written all over my heart. It has become as deep as the marrow in my bones.

SHEILA WALSH

Meditations on
Deep-rooted Hope

Christ was chosen before the creation of the world, but was revealed in these last times for your sake. Through him you believe in God, who raised him from the dead and glorified him, and so your faith and hope are in God.

❧ 1 Peter 1:20–21

Because God wanted to make the unchanging nature of his purpose very clear to the heirs of what was promised, he confirmed it with an oath. God did this so that, by two unchangeable things in which it is impossible for God to lie, we who have fled to take hold of the hope offered to us may be greatly encouraged. We have this hope as an anchor for the soul, firm and secure.

❧ Hebrews 6:17–19

Oh, How God Loves Us!

❧

*S*ometimes I think, *Who am I to be sharing my life story? I haven't arrived; I'm still in the middle of my journey!* But I have learned so much over the last five years of my life that I would never change the path the Lord took me on. The suffering—being brought to the end of yourself—is what prepared me to comfort others.

If you have pain in your heart over a loss, don't be embarrassed; don't let anyone pressure you to get through it and get on with your life. If you have the pain of loss, don't stuff it down and avoid it; experience it, but don't experience it alone. Reach out to receive comfort from someone who has been through it. Then, in time, you, too, will be able to comfort others with the comfort you receive from God.

◼ JAN DRAVECKY

*A*s I stood on stage and sang the words to my song, "God Is Faithful," I had a whole new appreciation for the many ways those words are true. Standing behind me were girls who just a year before were addicted to crack cocaine, living rough on the streets, in danger every night. Now they stood in lovely evening dresses and sang of the faithfulness of God. As the evening progressed, several teens stepped forward to share some of their stories. Woven through the heartbreak of their tales was a common thread: each girl and boy said they first encountered the love of God in the eyes of a woman named Sara Trollinger.

We all can't do what Sara does. But wherever God has placed us, let us pray that the grace of God is so rich in us that everything we say and do will shout the message, "Come, let me show you how God loves you."

SHEILA WALSH

Meditations on How God Loves Us

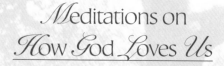

*H*ow great is the love the Father has lavished on us, that we should be called children of God!

&❧ 1 John 3:1

*T*he LORD is compassionate and gracious, slow to anger, abounding in love.

&❧ Psalm 103:8

*W*e know and rely on the love God has for us. God is love. Whoever lives in love lives in God, and God in him.

&❧ 1 John 4:16

*T*his is love: not that we loved God, but that he loved us and sent his Son as an atoning sacrifice for our sins.

&❧ 1 John 4:10

Share Kindness

✦

Small graces make the world go 'round. We receive these blessings from both strangers and friends: a neighbor who occasionally cleans the whole block with his snowblower; friends who come to our children's school performances and rave about how good they are (even if they aren't!); someone who breaks the tie in a store line by smiling and motioning for you to go first; the guy on the block who always buys the fund-raising candy, or sausage and cheese, or magazines from the middle school kids . . . people who give compliments; a stranger who says "puppy" instead of old dog, or "baby" instead of "ma'am."

What would the world be like without such kindnesses? Small kindnesses are more than they appear to be. Small kindnesses are small loves, small pieces of someone's caring.

VALERIE BELL

Meditations for Sharing Kindness

Dear friends, let us love one another for love comes from God.

> 1 John 4:7

Be kind and compassionate to one another.

> Ephesians 4:32

The fruit of the spirit is love, joy, peace, patience, kindness, goodness, faithfulness, gentleness and self-control. Against such things there is no law.

> Galatians 5:22–23

As God's chosen people, holy and dearly loved, clothe yourselves with compassion, kindness, humility, gentleness and patience. Bear with each other and forgive whatever grievances you may have against one another. Forgive as the Lord forgave you.

> Colossians 3:12–13

May the God of hope fill you with all joy and peace as you trust in him, so that you may overflow with hope by the power of the Holy Spirit.

    ❧ Romans 15:13

Do not throw away your confidence; it will be richly rewarded. You need to persevere so that when you have done the will of God, you will receive what he has promised.

    ❧ Hebrews 10:35–36

We have put our hope in the living God, who is the Savior of all men, especially of those who believe.

    ❧ 1 Timothy 4:10

Hope
for
Tomorrow

God Will Walk Us Through

*O*ne of my favorite words in the English language is *through*. I love it not for the way it sounds or the way it looks but for its meaning. It means "from beginning to end." That conveys encouragement to me.

On the morning my husband, Ken, died, what struck me as he took his final breath was that I could walk only so far through the experience with him. Earthbound limits were placed on me. I was, in essence, stuck here. The only one able to walk through the valley with Ken was the Shepherd. The eternal truth, "You are with me," from Psalm 23 can be ascribed only to God.

I find that truth comforting. Yes, the word *through* means there will be an end to whatever is happening with me on this earth. But an even greater promise in that word is that, when God walks me through, he suffers no human limitation; there is no separation from him. While God is with me in all my earthly "throughs," I'm heading for that final walk through, and we're doing it together.

■ MARILYN MEBERG

I learned for myself that the path out of the valley of depression is slow and laborious. From the time of my first panic attack in 1990, it took me over five years to recover, and I can't tell how long I was depressed before I had to face up to it and find help. Many times, storm clouds rolled over the mountains and drenched me in showers of tears. Many times, I almost missed the beams of hope gleaming through the black clouds.

But in the mountains, after the storms pass, the air is fresh, the sky, a clean translucent blue. Wildflowers that were watered by the rains paint the fields with brilliant colors as far as the eye can see. Like Solomon, I can say, "See! The winter is past; the rains are over. Flowers appear on the earth; the season of singing has come."

That is what I see in my life now: a fresh newness, a springlike beauty and joy. Through the valleys of depression and the storms of tears, the promises of God have proven true in my life.

JAN DRAVECKY

Meditation on God Will Walk Us Through

The LORD is my shepherd, I shall not be in
want.
He makes me lie down in green pastures,
he leads me beside quiet waters,
he restores my soul.
He guides me in paths of righteousness
for his name's sake.
Even though I walk
through the valley of the shadow of death,
I will fear no evil,
for you are with me;
your rod and your staff,
they comfort me.
You prepare a table before me
in the presence of my enemies.
You anoint my head with oil;
my cup overflows.
Surely goodness and love will follow me
all the days of my life,
and I will dwell in the house of the LORD
forever.

Psalm 23

Reverses and Setbacks

When we abandon ourselves to hopelessness we remove ourselves from Christ, our only hope—like the lemmings, who hurl themselves from a cliff into the sea.

Augustine said that our hearts are restless until they rest in God, but we try all sorts of things to still that pounding in our heads and the ache in our souls. Our impatience to have God move now, to act in ways that make sense to us, will drive us to take control of our lives. God is moving in ways that we cannot see or understand. This means we are left with the question, "Do I trust him?" We can choose to bow the knee now and ask him to forgive us for trying to squeeze the answer we want out of heaven, or we will bow the knee later in remorse at our foolishness in thinking that we knew better than God.

We are all thirsty in different ways, deep down in our souls. It is a thirst as ancient as the hills. But it is a thirst that can be satisfied only in Christ.

SHEILA WALSH

*S*ome of us are learning that cares are the tools God uses to fashion us for better things. He uses reverses to move us forward. Reverses and cares bow us down low until we finally drop to our knees. But a lot of kneeling keeps us in good standing because it brings us closer to God. Being close to God, we find peace. Even if our cares aren't resolved as we wish and even if we finally have to admit life in this world will never be safe or predictable, we may discover that's because we were made for another place.

BARBARA JOHNSON

Meditations on Reverses and Setbacks

My soul thirsts for God, for the living God. When can I go and meet with God? . . . Why are you downcast, O my soul? Why so disturbed within me? Put your hope in God, for I will yet praise him, my Savior and my God.

   ❦ Psalm 42:2, 5–6

We are hard pressed on every side, but not crushed; perplexed, but not in despair; persecuted, but not abandoned; struck down, but not destroyed.

   ❦ 2 Corinthians 4:8–9

You will be secure, because there is hope; you will look about you and take your rest in safety.

   ❦ Job 11:18

Rock-Solid Hope

*W*hen we face death, when we face the loss of loved ones, we desperately need a rock-solid hope. The thought that this life is all there is—that we live and then die—is dreadful. When you realize how fragile life is, you search hard for the truth. You have to know what is real. You need a hope beyond this life.

JAN DRAVECKY

*B*ehind the cloud the starlight lurks,
    Through showers the sunbeams fall;
For God, who loveth all His works,
    Has left His hope for all.

JOHN GREENLEAF WHITTIER

*R*eal mourning is ugly and deep and wrenching, no matter how flowery and tasteful sympathy cards try to make it out to be. But trying to sidestep grief represents a proud and silly effort to avoid the unavoidable. When Jesus promised that those who mourn would be comforted, he laid down an inescapable prerequisite for receiving the deep, rich wonder of God's healing. To become a candidate for his comfort, you first must open yourself up to the pain of mourning.

Paul told his fellow believers not to grieve hopelessly, but he did not challenge them to forego grieving. Grief is different for a follower of Christ. Even in the depths of sorrow, hope breathes. Hope that you will see your loved one again in heaven. Hope in God's capacity to infuse suffering with purpose. And hope that because of his healing power, your sorrow will not go on forever.

MAUREEN RANK

Meditations on a Rock-Solid Hope

The Lord *is good to those whose hope is in him, to the one who seeks him; it is good to wait quietly for the salvation of the* Lord.

Lamentations 3:25–26

Jesus said, "Blessed are those who mourn, for they will be comforted."

Matthew 5:4

I love you, O Lord, *my strength. The* Lord *is my rock, my fortress and my deliverer; my God is my rock, in whom I take refuge. He is my shield and the horn of my salvation, my stronghold.*

Psalm 18:1–2

Those who sow in tears will reap with songs of joy. He who goes out weeping, carrying seed to sow, will return with songs of joy, carrying sheaves with him.

Psalm 126:5–6

God Is Already There

So how do we continue to make good choices and enjoy God's grace in the midst of tough times? Well, first we have to make a habit of drinking deeply of the grace God promises, every moment. The apostle Paul knew the secret: "But he said to me, 'My grace is sufficient for you, for my power is made perfect in weakness.' Therefore I will boast all the more gladly about my weaknesses, so that Christ's power may rest on me. That is why, for Christ's sake, I delight in weaknesses, in insults, in hardships, in persecutions, in difficulties. For when I am weak, then I am strong" (2 Corinthians 12:9–10). God's grace is here, now. We just have to uncover our soul and let grace soak us to our roots.

SHEILA WALSH

My friend, remember to take this life one day at a time. When several days attack you, don't give up. A successful woman takes the bricks the Devil throws at her and uses them to lay a firm foundation. We all need enough trials to challenge us, enough challenges to strengthen us, and enough strength to do our part in making this a better place to live and love. Grace is receiving the gift of God in exactly who we are and bearing its fruit in the world. Just think how it changed the world because Noah didn't say, "I don't do arks." Paul didn't say, "I don't do letters." Martin Luther didn't say, "I don't do doors." And, of course, Jesus didn't say, "I don't do crosses."

Some people can't afford the tuition for the school of hard knocks. But that's where grace comes in. When God believes in you, your situation is never hopeless. When he walks with you, you are never alone. When God is on your side, you can never *ever* lose. So don't be afraid of tomorrow; God is already there!

BARBARA JOHNSON

Meditations for God Is Already There

God's solid foundation stands firm, sealed with this inscription: "The Lord knows those who are his."

       2 Timothy 2:19

When I am afraid, I will trust in you. In God, whose word I praise, in God I trust; I will not be afraid.

       Psalm 56:3–4

I have set the LORD always before me. Because he is at my right hand, I will not be shaken.

       Psalm 16:8

Tell the righteous it will be well with them, for they will enjoy the fruit of their deeds.

       Isaiah 3:10

Thinking About Heaven

❧

There's nothing escapist about pondering heaven. Jesus told us about it not so that we could escape from our troubles but so that we could better endure them. He wants us to think about heaven, especially when anxious thoughts seize our hearts. Although we won't enjoy its full benefits until we arrive, even now we can allow its atmosphere to fill our lungs with hope.

Thinking about heaven is a great way to put "all that stuff" behind us, at least for a little while. Jesus wanted us to know that, when the time is right, there won't be any problem in getting us to heaven. He wouldn't entrust this task to some third-level angel or to some celestial scoop that would mechanically pluck us out of earth and dump us in paradise. He wanted us to know that he would come for us himself.

DAVE AND JAN DRAVECKY

Be thou my Vision, O Lord of my heart;
Naught be all else to me save that thou art—
Thou my best thought by day or by night,
Waking or sleeping, thy presence my light.

Riches I need not, nor man's empty praise,
Thou my inheritance, now and always;
Thou and Thou only, first in my heart,
High King of heaven, my Treasure thou art.

High King of heaven, my victory won,
May I reach heaven's joys, O bright heav'n's
    Sun!
Heart of my own heart, whatever befall,
Still be my Vision, O Ruler of all.

GAELIC HYMN
TRANSLATED BY MARY BYRNE

Meditations on Thinking About Heaven

No eye has seen, no ear has heard, no mind has conceived what God has prepared for those who love him.

    🌿 1 Corinthians 2:9

The angel carried me away in the Spirit to a mountain great and high, and showed me the Holy City, Jerusalem, coming down out of heaven from God. It shone with the glory of God, and its brilliance was like that of a very precious jewel, like a jasper, clear as crystal.... I did not see a temple in the city, because the Lord God Almighty and the Lamb are its temple. The city does not need the sun or the moon to shine on it, for the glory of God gives it light, and the Lamb is its lamp.... On no day will its gates ever be shut, for there will be no night there.... Then the angel showed me the river of the water of life, as clear as crystal, flowing from the throne of God and of the Lamb down the middle of the great street of the city.

    🌿 Revelation 21:10–11, 22–23,25,

22:1–2

Don't Give Up

It's hard to let go of things in which we have placed our hope—even when they lie broken in our hands. It's even harder to let go of our preconceived ideas of how God works when those lie shattered at our feet.

Many of us carry around a heavy weight of discouragement. It seems as if nothing will ever get any better, nothing will change. In the midst of that I offer these words of hope, of promise: "God is faithful; he will not let you be tempted beyond what you can bear" (1 Corinthians 10:13).

Perhaps it seems to you that you are at the breaking point. I urge you in the name of the Lord to throw yourself on him, to hide yourself under his wings. Don't give up. You have come too far. The road ahead may look bleak, but trust in God. It is the way home.

SHEILA WALSH

I have learned that God is faithful, even in the midst of cancer. He is faithful, even in the middle of amputation. He is faithful throughout the pain, the suffering, the doubts, the worries, the sleepless nights. When Peter tells us that "those who suffer according to God's will should commit themselves to their faithful Creator and continue to do good," I know it's outstanding advice.

Suffering comes for all sorts of reasons: We make bad health choices; Satan afflicts us; God wants to use our suffering to glorify him. But in the end, if you're a believer, God wants to redeem your suffering and use it for good, somehow. He is a faithful Creator, so we must trust him. We do not yet know how he plans to use our suffering to display his glory before a breathless universe, but we know that's what he's up to. And that's true whether we recover or we don't, whether we live or we die. We just don't know how such a faithful Creator will use our suffering for his glory, but he has said that he will.

DAVE AND JAN DRAVECKY

Meditations on
Don't Give Up

*L*et us not become weary in doing good, for at the proper time we will reap a harvest if we do not give up.

Galatians 6:9

*B*e strong and do not give up, for your work will be rewarded.

2 Chronicles 15:7

I have fought the good fight, I have finished the race, I have kept the faith. Now there is in store for me the crown of righteousness, which the Lord, the righteous Judge, will award to me on that day—and not only to me, but also to all who have longed for his appearing.

2 Timothy 4:7–8

Tremendous Peace

❦

I can't begin to answer the question of why God does what he does in ways that I consider a bit off-kilter and odd, but I can certainly describe the lessons I learn from these methods. These lessons contribute a tremendous peace and soul satisfaction when fully understood. My peace is bolstered when I contemplate as well as experience God's totally unfathomable workings in my life. That's because I know for a fact that he's around! There's no other explanation for how things are going . . . or not going. Sometimes his odd working gets my attention to the point of whiplashing me into a neck brace! My response is always "who but God?" When I have a "who but God" reaction, I know who to credit for whatever is going on in my life—and that assurance produces peace.

Not only do these peculiar methods get my attention and cause me to focus on him rather than on myself, but I am also reminded that God does what he does to underscore who he is.

🌿 MARILYN MEBERG

*M*y brother Chuck says, "Hope doesn't require a massive chain where heavy links of logic hold it together. A thin wire will do . . . just strong enough to get us through the night until the wind dies down." Hope is a heartfelt assurance that our heavenly Father knows what's best for us and never makes a mistake. God says, "Trust me. Remember my Word. Believe . . . and wait."

Of course, our greatest hope lies waiting for us at the end of time, when all God's purposes will be fulfilled. We will go to live with Jesus Christ, who by his grace redeemed us, loved us through our trials, provided joy in the midst of heartache, peace for our troubled hearts, and freedom from a boring lifestyle. We'll be with him forever—an outrageous reality!

LUCI SWINDOLL

Meditations on Tremendous Peace

The LORD bless you and keep you; the LORD make his face shine upon you and be gracious to you; the LORD turn his face toward you and give you peace.

Numbers 6:24–26

Great peace have they who love your law, and nothing can make them stumble.

Psalm 119:165

Therefore, since we have been justified through faith, we have peace with God through our Lord Jesus Christ.

Romans 5:1

The fruit of righteousness will be peace; the effect of righteousness will be quietness and confidence forever.

Isaiah 32:17

Looking Heavenward

❧

*W*hen we finally realize that the hopes we have cherished will never come true, that a loved one is gone from this life forever, that a child's diagnosis of inoperable cancer will never change, or that we will never be as successful as we had once imagined, our sights are lifted heavenward.

JONI EARECKSON TADA

If God hath made this world so fair
Where sin and death abound,
How beautiful beyond compare
Will paradise be found.

JAMES MONTGOMERY

*O*ur heart is in heaven, our home is not here.

REGINALD HEBER

*G*od may never answer our question "How long?" He may never tell us how much farther we must trudge through the desert. But if our wilderness journey leads us to him, then the road we travel is as surely a highway to heaven as is any more rapid thoroughfare. Who knows when the trip will be over? Maybe tomorrow, maybe next week, or next year. God does not give us an ETA, an Estimated Time of Arrival. But if we belong to him, he does give us a GTA—a Guaranteed Territory of Arrival. And from what we can glimpse in the official travel brochure of his Word, the place is spectacular.

DAVE AND JAN DRAVECKY

Meditations on Looking Heavenward

*W*ho have I in heaven but you?
And earth has nothing I desire
besides you. My flesh and my heart
may fail but God is the strength of
my heart and my portion forever.

⃠ Psalm 73:25–26

*F*or the grace of God that brings
salvation . . . teaches us to say "No"
to ungodliness and worldly passions,
and to live self-controlled, upright
and godly lives in this present age,
while we wait for the blessed hope—
the glorious appearing of our great
God and Savior, Jesus Christ.

⃠ Titus 2:11–13

God Wins!

❧

God doesn't command us to stay encouraged without giving us a reason to do so. He knows there is plenty in life to cause even the stoutest soul to lose heart. Calamities and mishaps and disease and accidents and foul play and a thousand other devastations can pulverize our lives at any moment. Life in this fallen world has countless nasty ways of causing us to lose heart.

But God is greater than any calamity, mightier than any disaster. When Paul says, "Therefore we do not lose heart," he is thinking back to an irresistible reason for staying encouraged: "We know that the one who raised the Lord Jesus from the dead will also raise us with Jesus and present us with you in his presence."

Death does not have the final say—Jesus does! And so long as we are connected to Jesus by faith, death has no more say over us than it did over him. Truly, this is the most powerful reason in the universe for taking heart, no matter what happens. God wins! And we win with him.

DAVE AND JAN DRAVECKY

*O*n one day, in the instant it takes for a car and truck to collide, six college classmates died. These weren't anonymous men and women; I knew each of them. When they died I was hundreds of miles away taking classes at another university. Alone, I had no one to share my grief, to hold me when I sobbed. Grieving for six tore me apart.

Loving sets us up for sorrow, that's true. But it also encourages us to hope. Although I didn't understand it immediately, I grew to realize that the affection I had for these classmates had grown from a foundation of common faith. On such a foundation my hope began to flourish. What we had most in common was the very thing that assured me of their well-being. Because of the resurrection, the horror of death melted away. I would see them again.

I can't help but grieve when I look at some of the photographs in my college yearbooks. But I have hope because I know that "death has been swallowed up in victory." Jesus Christ is the victor!

MARTHA MANIKAS-FOSTER

Meditations on God Wins!

When the perishable has been clothed with the imperishable, and the mortal with immortality, then the saying that is written will come true: "Death has been swallowed up in victory. Where, O death, is your victory? Where, O death, is your sting?" The sting of death is sin, and the power of sin is the law. But thanks be to God! He gives us the victory through our Lord Jesus Christ.

      1 Corinthians 15:54–57

We do not want you to be ignorant about those who fall asleep, or to grieve like the rest of men, who have no hope. We believe that Jesus died and rose again and so we believe that God will bring with Jesus those who have fallen asleep in him.

      1 Thessalonians 4:13–14

Jesus said, "You will weep and mourn while the world rejoices. You will grieve, but your grief will turn to joy."

      John 16:20

God Understands Our Suffering

R. C. Sproul said, "No one was ever called by God to greater suffering than that suffering to which God called His only begotten son. Our Savior was a suffering Savior. He went before us into the uncharted land of agony and death."

When suffering invades their lives, many complain, "God doesn't understand!" But he does. He understands it far better than we do. Our Savior suffered vastly more than we will ever begin to grasp—and he did it for our sake.

DAVE AND JAN DRAVECKY

*G*od and I. That was it. In the face of death, it's either that or nothing at all. There was no one to blame, no sign, no certainty, no cure in sight, and no telling what God had in mind. I was really frightened. Death is, for me, the great intruder.

I was angry with God that he would ask me even to consider it. I had questions for which I didn't think God had the answers, or if he did, he wasn't willing to share them with me. And when I asked those questions, a surprising thing happened: what was meant as confrontation became release. Far from resenting my questions, God welcomed them. He bore the pain in the questions just as Christ bore the cross. In my confusion, I may have wanted to wound him, but he only bled for me. In expressing what was really going on inside me—the anger, the hurt, the rage against dying—he comprehended my pain and translated my helplessness into certain strength. In the release of control, I have found humbling power. In the chaos, I have found moments of sustaining peace.

DEFORIA LANE

Meditations on God Understands Our Suffering

Surely [the Messiah] took up our infirmities and carried our sorrows, yet we considered him stricken by God, smitten by him, and afflicted. But he was pierced for our transgressions, he was crushed for our iniquities; the punishment that brought us peace was upon him, and by his wounds we are healed.

 ✿ Isaiah 53:4–5

Let us fix our eyes on Jesus, the author and perfecter of our faith, who for the joy set before him endured the cross, scorning its shame, and sat down at the right hand of the throne of God. Consider him who endured such opposition from sinful men, so that you will not grow weary and lose heart.

 ✿ Hebrews 12:2–3

What Heaven Is Like

❧

What will heaven be like? If you talk to people about it, you can hear as many interpretations of heaven as people you ask. It seems that everyone has his or her own expectations of what it is going to be like.

We had guests over one night. It had been an evening of laughter. Our talk turned lightly to what heaven might be like. My extroverted husband, Steve, said that heaven would be like a giant beach party and all of his friends would be there. . . . When it was my turn I said I pictured heaven to be like living on an African safari, except all the animals would be tame and you would not have to feed or clean up after them. They laughed at me and called me "Sheena of Heaven." . . .

When we came to our guest's small son, he looked up with an innocent expression, his face covered with a chocolate-cake smile, and said, "I think heaven is going to be . . . whenever you want . . . you can get up in Jesus' lap!"

VALERIE BELL

*W*hat is your vision of heaven? What are you hoping for? I used to picture my life in eternity as . . . well, a bit dull. I mean, what would I do all day? Once I had chatted with all the great heroes of the faith and had a good look around to see who made it and who didn't, then what? Would it just be two million rounds of "Kum Ba Yah"?

I'm amazed that God doesn't just slap me around sometimes. I'm so small-minded; I have the vision of a housefly. And yet in his grace and outrageous love he keeps talking to me and letting me in on the big picture. We are told that now we see through a glass darkly, but then we will see face-to-face. It's as if all our lives the only reflection we've had of ourselves and each other is the distorted image in a fun-house mirror; but when that day comes, the distorted images will be gone, everything crooked made straight, everything snapped back into place.

SHEILA WALSH

191

Meditations on What Heaven Is Like

They were longing for a better country—a heavenly one. Therefore God is not ashamed to be called their God, for he has prepared a city for them.

🍀 Hebrews 11:16

The wall of the city [of heaven] had twelve foundations, and on them were the names of the twelve apostles of the Lamb. . . . The wall was made of jasper, and the city of pure gold, as pure as glass. The foundations of the city walls were decorated with every kind of precious stone. The first foundation was jasper, the second sapphire, the third chalcedony, the fourth emerald, the fifth sardonyx, the sixth carnelian, the seventh chrysolite, the eighth beryl, the ninth topaz, the tenth chrysoprase, the eleventh jacinth, and the twelfth amethyst. The twelve gates were twelve pearls, each gate made of a single pearl. The great street of the city was of pure gold, like transparent glass.

🍀 Revelation 21:14, 18–21

Hope for All Your Days

*W*hat does hope really look like? You might wonder. When your precious teenager is addicted to drugs or your best friend is mad at you or your four-year-old is driving you crazy with her center-stageism, where does hope come in? Let me suggest three practical ways to make it real in your life.

Accept your reality. I don't know anybody who likes what she does or where she is every minute of the day. But the reality is, we are where we are, and God is doing something right here, whether we see it or not. He wastes nothing. He's growing us up in himself.

Bring God into your reality. Bringing God into your reality means being fully present in the moment—not wishing you were somewhere you used to be or somewhere you hope to be.

Make life an adventure. Ask God for a fresh perspective on your life. Try things you've never tried before. Ask yourself what you want most from life, and go for it.

Luci Swindoll

I recently heard hope described so vividly by my pastor, Barry John Lyons, Sr. He said that people who have a relationship with Jesus and who understand the implications of their salvation through him can rest in their hope like babes in arms. Salvation is three-dimensional, he said: past, present, future. In the past we were saved from the penalty of sin; in the present we are saved from the power of sin; in the future we will be saved from the punishment of sin. When we repent, believe, and receive Jesus Christ as our personal Savior, we are justified, found "not guilty" in the sight of God. Then we are sanctified, one day at a time, as the Holy Spirit within us changes our hearts and we respond by doing more right than wrong. When we die we will be glorified, never to hope for more! We will finally be at home in hope, forever.

THELMA WELLS

Meditations on Hope for All Your Days

Though you have not seen Christ, you love him; and even though you do not see him now, you believe in him and are filled with an inexpressible and glorious joy, for you are receiving the goal of your faith, the salvation of your souls.

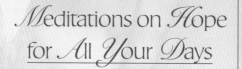 1 Peter 1:8–9

For God so loved the world that he gave his one and only Son, that whoever believes in him shall not perish but have eternal life.

John 3:16

The Perfect Body

❧

*O*ur hope as Christians can never be placed on refurbishing or gussying up our present bodies. You can spend all your time and money on that pursuit if you want to, but in the end you're going to end up looking like the bald man who tries to conceal his shiny scalp with a long wisp of side hair twirled on top of his still-gleaming dome. Nobody is fooled, and you've wasted your efforts.

I don't have time for that nonsense, because I'm getting a brand-new body that comes complete with everything I need. That means a lot to a man who's missing an arm and a shoulder. In the past few years I've met dozens of people who have lost arms or legs or feet or hands, who have been damaged physically, whether through accident, disease, birth defects, or old age. These folks are looking forward to their new bodies every bit as much as I am. They know what it is to be physically limited now, and they can't wait to find out what their new bodies will have to offer.

DAVE DRAVECKY

*T*he new body that we will have will be a glorious body like the body of Christ. It will be an eternal body. It will never know tears, heartache, tragedy, disease, suffering, death, or fatigue. It will be a renewed body, but still recognizable.

BILLY GRAHAM

*H*eaven's the perfection of all that can be said or thought—riches, delight, harmony, health, beauty; and all these not subject to the waste of time, but in their height eternal.

JAMES SHIRLEY

Meditations on the Perfect Body

God has made everything beautiful in its time. He has also set eternity in the hearts of men; yet they cannot fathom what God has done from beginning to end.

&⁊ Ecclesiastes 3:11

Our citizenship is in heaven. And we eagerly await a Savior from there, the Lord Jesus Christ, who, by the power that enables him to bring everything under his control, will transform our lowly bodies so that they will be like his glorious body.

&⁊ Philippians 3:20–21

The body that is sown is perishable, it is raised imperishable; it is sown in dishonor, it is raised in glory; it is sown in weakness, it is raised in power; it is sown a natural body, it is raised a spiritual body.

&⁊ 1 Corinthians 15:42–44

Part of the Process

❧

To the majority of people, through most of their lives, death is seen as an enemy, an event to be dreaded because of the traumatic separations and endings it imposes on human life. Once a person comes to realize that death is not final, but is a part of the process, the fear and sorrow is greatly reduced. For the person who suffers and for those who live with the sufferer, an understanding of life after death brings great comfort. Death is not just the end of the pain, but is also the release into a new life free of pain.

R. C. SPROUL

*W*e would never make light of the suffering that people endure here on earth. No pain *feels* "light and momentary" while we are in its throes. There is no comparing pain, either; everyone suffers differently and uniquely. What is extremely painful to one person may be no pain at all to another.

There is great comfort in knowing that our suffering will come to an end, that "this too shall pass." And there is even greater comfort in know that "glory" awaits. This is the divine trade we make, an exchange of all that we have in return for all that God has. I'm not sure what he gets out of the deal, but it's one I wouldn't dream of turning down.

DAVE AND JAN DRAVECKY

Meditations on
Part of the Process

I consider that our present suffer-ings are not worth comparing with the glory that will be revealed in us.

❧ Romans 8:18

God did not appoint us to suffer wrath but to receive salvation through our Lord Jesus Christ. He died for us so that . . . we may live together with him.

❧ 1 Thessalonians 5:9–10

Dear friends, do not be surprised at the painful trial you are suffering, as though something strange were happening to you. But rejoice that you participate in the sufferings of Christ, so that you may be overjoyed when his glory is revealed.

❧ 1 Peter 4:12–13

Glorious Hope

❧

When you welcome God's companionship in the darkest hours of your life, when you keep on walking by faith on the darker parts of the path, you are gifted with moments of wonderful elation—as if you are joining with heaven in a celebration that is a tiny shadow of what it will be like when we get home. The closer we push into the heart of God, the more we are swept away by the joy that is his breath and life and gift to us all.

SHEILA WALSH

Hope, like the gleaming taper's light
Adorns and cheers our way;
And still, as darker grows the night,
Emits a brighter ray.

OLIVER GOLDSMITH

*J*esus knew everything that was coming. And yet he had the audacity—or was it the authority?—to say, *no one will take away your joy.*

And now for the really good news: His promise belongs as much to you as it did to the disciples! Why? Because he based it on a single, priceless fact: "I will see you again." Do you share that conviction? Then so will you share the promise. As surely as one day the Lord will greet each of his children, so surely will he immerse us in his joy—a joy that no one will take away.

But, Lord, I'm in such pain!
No one will take away your joy.

But the doctors have given up hope!
No one will take away your joy.

But my whole world feels like it's caving in!
No one will take away your joy.

That is our hope. That is the glorious hope promised us. And that is the hope that is able to see us through all of our tears, all of our groans, and all of our grief.

It's as certain as the promise of Jesus.

DAVE AND JAN DRAVECKY

Meditations on Glorious Hope

Jesus said, "Now is your time of grief, but I will see you again and you will rejoice, and no one will take away your joy."

🌿 John 16:22

I heard a loud voice from the throne saying, "Now the dwelling of God is with men, and he will live with them. They will be his people, and God himself will be with them and be their God. He will wipe every tear from their eyes. There will be no more death or mourning or crying or pain, for the old order of things has passed away."

🌿 Revelation 21:3–4

Be strong and take heart, all you who hope in the LORD.

🌿 Psalm 31:24

*L*et us hold unswervingly to the hope we profess for God who promised is faithful.

❧ Hebrews 10:23

*F*or I know the plans I have for you," declares the LORD, "plans to prosper you and not to harm you, plans to give you hope and a future. Then you will call upon me and come and pray to me, and I will listen to you."

❧ Jeremiah 29:11–12

God Is in Every Tomorrow

God is in every tomorrow,
    Therefore I live for today;
Certain of finding at sunrise
    Guidance and strength for the day,
Power for each moment of weakness,
    Hope for each moment of pain
Comfort for every sorrow,
    Sunshine and joy after rain.

God is in every tomorrow,
    Planning for you and for me,
E'en in the dark I will follow,
    Trust where my eyes cannot see,

Stilled by His promise of blessing,
    Soothed by the touch of His hand,
Confident in His protection,
    Knowing my life-path is planned.

God is in every tomorrow,
    Life with its changes may come,
He is behind and before me,
    While in the distance shines Home.
Home—where no thoughts of tomorrow
    Ever can shadow my brow,
Home in the presence of Jesus,
    Through all Eternity now!

AUTHOR UNKNOWN

EXCERPTS TAKEN FROM:

Buchanan, Sue. *Duh-votions*. Copyright 1999 by Sue Buchanan. Grand Rapids, MI: ZondervanPublishingHouse, 1999.

Bell, Valerie. *A Well-Tended Soul*. Copyright 1996 by Valerie Bell. Grand Rapids, MI: ZondervanPublishingHouse, 1996.

Clairmont, Patsy, Barbara Johnson, Marilyn Meberg, Luci Swindoll, Sheila Walsh, Thelma Wells. *Extravagant Grace*. Copyright 2000 by Women of Faith, Inc. Grand Rapids, MI: ZondervanPublishing House, 2000. *Outrageous Joy*. Copyright 1999 by Women of Faith, Inc. Grand Rapids, MI: ZondervanPublishingHouse, 1999. *Overjoyed*. Copyright 1999 by Women of Faith, Inc. Grand Rapids, MI: ZondervanPublishingHouse, 1999.

Dravecky, Dave and Jan with Amanda Sorenson. *Glimpses of Heaven*. Copyright 1998 by David and Janice Dravecky. Grand Rapids, MI: ZondervanPublishingHouse, 1998.

Dravecky, Dave and Jan with Steve Halliday. *Do Not Lose Heart*. Copyright 1998 by David and Janice Dravecky. Grand Rapids, MI: ZondervanPublishingHouse, 1998.

Dravecky, Jan with Connie Neal. *A Joy I'd Never Known*. Copyright 1996 by Janice Dravecky. Grand Rapids, MI: ZondervanPublishing House, 1996.

Meberg, Marilyn. *Choosing the Amusing*. Copyright 1999 by Word Publishing. Published by Word Publishing, a Thomas Nelson Company. All rights reserved.

Meberg, Marilyn. *I'd Rather Be Laughing*. Copyright 1998 by Marilyn Meberg. Published by Word Publishing. All rights reserved.

Spangler, Ann, compiler. *She Who Laughs, Lasts!* Copyright 2000 by Ann Spangler. Grand Rapids, MI: ZondervanPublishingHouse, 2000.

Walsh, Sheila. *Gifts for Your Soul*. Copyright 1997 by Sheila Walsh. Grand Rapids MI: ZondervanPublishingHouse, 1997.

Women's Devotional Bible 2. Copyright 1995 by the Zondervan Corporation. Grand Rapids, MI: ZondervanPublishingHouse, 1995.

Women's Devotional Bible. Copyright 1990 by the Zondervan Corporation. Grand Rapids, MI: ZondervanPublishingHouse, 1990.